The Cannabible 2

The Cannabible 2

Jason
King

TEN SPEED PRESS
Berkeley | Toronto

Author's Note

Though I would love for every volume of *The Cannabible* to feature all strains of marijuana from certain geographic locations, the nature of the kind makes this less than possible. What I mean by this is that there will always be new and old strains that I will come across from California, for example. If I had put all California strains in the first volume of *The Cannabible*, then I would never get to show you all the new California strains I've found in the years since. This would be unacceptable. Therefore, *The Cannabibles* will contain new strains as I find them in my travels.

I'd also like to mention that some readers will notice that I have included very little information about growth characteristics and expected harvest sizes. This is because this subject is completely subjective. For example, a strain could be grown indoors using a Sea of Green method and yield a half ounce per plant. That same strain grown outdoors in full sunlight might yield three pounds. For the strains included in *The Cannabibles* that are sold by seed companies, you can easily obtain this type of information on their websites or catalogs, as well as a number of other websites.

Lastly, all of the information presented is as accurate, to my knowledge, as possible. However, I welcome futher information that you may have on any of the included strains. To contact me, send an email to cannabible@hotmail.com.

Ten Speed Press
P.O. Box 7123
Berkeley, California 94707
www.tenspeed.com

Distributed in Canada by Ten Speed Press Canada, in New Zealand by Southern Publishers Group, in South Africa by Real Books, and in the United Kingdom and Europe by Airlift Book Company.

Cover and Text Design: Toni Tajima
Digital production artist: Mona Meisami

Library of Congress Cataloging-in-Publication Data
   King, Jason, 1971–
      The cannabible 2 / Jason King.
         p. cm.
      ISBN 1-58008-516-4 (pbk.) — ISBN 1-58008-517-2 (hardcover)
      1. Cannabis. 2. Marijuana. I. Title.
      SB295.C35 K56 2003
      633.5'3—dc21   2001004451

First printing, 2003

Printed in China

1 2 3 4 5 6 7 8 9 10 — 06 05 04 03

This book is dedicated to the Cannabis Devas, the nature spirits associated with the cannabis plant. They are truly responsible for the stunning beauty of the cannabis plant, as well as its vast array of medicinal and recreational effects. Mahalo. Please read *The Secret Life of Nature*, by Peter Tompkins, if you wish to learn more about these amazing beings.

Acknowledgments

Many Mahalos to: Jah, Rebeca, Bob Marley, Joan Bello, Dave Frankel, Mediman, Francis, Robear, nc & C, Eddy Lepp, Nebu, Mark McCoy, Roger Christie, Jack Herer, Albert Hoffman, The Redneck Ridge Clan, JD, Chris Iverson, Woody Harrelson, George Soros, Dennis Peron, Dana Larsen, *Cannabis Culture* Magazine, Patanjali, JFJO, DJ Short, Sensi Seed Bank, Mullaway Seeds, Uncle Phil, Sista Annie Nelson, Toni T, Brother LeeRoy Campbell, Nimbin Hemp Embassy, Andrew Kavasilas, Dr. Milan Hopkins, and all the others who couldn't be named for obvious reasons.

Contents

How Does He Do It?
BY ROGER CHRISTIE

t o create *The Cannabible* takes the vision and hard work of the most dedicated natural scientist, photojournalist, and cannabis gourmet. Add the people skills needed in dealing with some of the most cautious, private, and paranoid gardeners on Earth, and the timing necessary to capture the peak photo opportunity in the famous flower's life, and it's clear *The Cannabible* represents the very best of the cannabis culture and breaks any remaining myth about cannabis use and motivation, memory, and getting the job done right. Just look at volume 1. It's heavy, glossy, gorgeous, and useful, too.

Jason's life on the cannabis trail for the last seven years and counting is much more than a job; it's an inspired, passionate, high-stakes adventure worthy of its own book and movie. Imagine what it might take for you to find, photograph, and enjoy some of the best strains of cannabis on Earth.

Each photo segment is unique. Jason must move to an area and set up house, sometimes for months. He makes friends and joins in the culture he has become so accustomed to since his memorable days and nights on the Grateful Dead tour.

Often it takes more than fifty pounds of cameras, lights, microscopes, and other necessities to carry in. He must set up all the equipment, outdoors or in, then wait for just the right moment, which could be midnight for an indoor grow, just before the lights come on, or sunup or sundown for the perfect natural light to shine on the glistening resin glands that are so highly prized the world over.

So sit back, light up, and enjoy a good book. Jason did the work so we don't have to. Pakaloha.

EDDY'S

Medicinal Gardens
& Chapel

NOTICE:
PRIVATE PROPERTY

Any person entering this private property **must hold contract** with owner and/or tenant which grants ingress with indemnity.

NO TRESPASS

INCLUDING ALL INDIVIDUALS, PUBLIC/CORPORATE OFFICIALS, THEIR AGENTS, EMPLOYEES or FRANCHISES THERE OF:
This puts you on NOTICE that the owner and/or tenant of this property requires that all Public/Corporate Officials, their Agents, Employees, or Franchises thereof abide by provisions of the **Supreme Law of the Land: The Constitution for the United States of America.**

<u>Trespasser</u>- One who intentionally and without consent enter another's property.

<u>Criminal Trespass</u>-Entering or remaining upon or in any land, structure, or transportation device when such premises or property are posted in a manner reasonably likely to come to the attention of intruders.

Acts done <u>under color of any law</u> carry the same restrictions as any other criminal trespass. USC Title 42, Sec. 1983

BE WARNED!! USC Title 18, Sec. 3109 STRICTLY ENFORCED!! (The owner of this property may use force to remove those who trespass!!!)

The Penalty for Trespass is a **fine of not more than $10,000 or imprisoned for not more than ten years, or both.** USC Title 18, Sec. 241 & 242.

Signature *Eddy*
Property Owner

STOP

IF I KNOW YOU'RE COMING,
COME ON UP.
IF I DON'T, <u>STOP</u> & <u>READ</u>
THE FUCKIN' SIGNS!
**Prohibida la Entrada
No Traspasar**

WELCOME TO EDDY'S MEDICINAL GARDE
& MULTI-DENOMINATIONAL MINISTRY
OF CANNABIS & RASTAFARI.

DO NOT ENTER WITHOUT APPOINTME

CALL 275-8879

Preface

august 2002. I'm in California, chasing the harvest, as usual. My days are spent cruising up and down the West Coast, finding the true connoisseurs in the area, and somehow talking them into letting me take pictures of their most private crop. According to the local growers, this is the best season California has had in twenty years. It hasn't rained in nearly a year, and the intense California sun is coaxing the local ganja crop to unbelievable sizes. Admittedly, the passage of Proposition 215, which legalized medical marijuana in California, is making my job much easier than before. Some days I drive over 300 miles and photograph three or more gardens.

Throughout the summer, I am repeatedly told of a legendary garden in Upper Lake, affectionately known as Eddy's Medicinal Garden. I am told there are hundreds of humongous ganja plants, over eighty different strains, some of the plants towering at well over fifteen feet tall. The plants, each large enough to harvest several pounds of herb, are supposedly being grown in full sunlight, within sight of a highway.

I also hear through the ganja vine of the ballsy Vietnam vet responsible for all these plants, a man by the name of Eddy Lepp. Having heard several descriptions of his bold and defiant character, I felt I knew and loved him before I even met him. This strange feeling was validated while at the Seattle Hemp Fest, when I heard a man in the background boasting about his garden being the best in the world, while proudly handing a person a giant "business card" with a picture of him and his wife in front of the monstrous plants. I walked up and introduced myself and said, "You *must* be Eddy Lepp."

"I sure am," he proudly replied.

We became friends instantly, and after he signed one of his cards to me, we agreed that I should extensively photograph his garden throughout the harvest season. Within days I made the journey to his land, about an hour and a half northeast of the San Francisco Bay. As I

approached from the freeway, I spotted a giant mass of thriving green forest in the distance. "That couldn't be it," I assured myself. But as I drew nearer, I was blown away when I realized and accepted the fact that this was in fact a giant ganja forest.

As I pulled up the driveway, I was greeted by a man on an ATV who kindly opened the more than substantial security gate for me. By this point, my heart was thumping noticeably in my chest, as I could already smell the kind bud. By the time I parked next to the garden, I could hardly walk. I threw open the door to my car and stumbled toward the garden, a sea of kind bud wafting in the breeze. Seeing Eddy waving me toward the garden out of the corner of my eye, I entered the maze of plants without hesitation. I felt dwarfed by these megaplants, neatly spaced about fifteen feet apart and filling all of the gaps. Several happy workers were tending to the plants, and the garden was pulsating with a loving and magnificent energy. I could feel the happiness of the devas, the spirits of the plants, working with these plants, stoked to be enjoying the full sunlight rather than hiding underneath other plants as so often is the case.

Every plant was in perfect health and neatly labeled with relevant strain and growth information. After several minutes literally lost in the maze of kind, I found Eddy and he began the

tour. This garden had no expenses spared. Everything was 100 percent organic. There were top Dutch strains, California strains, Swiss strains, and a few of Eddy's own strains, which honestly seemed the most impressive. Although most of the plants were over a month from harvest, colas literally the size of my torso were everywhere. Sexy slender sativas, pungent acrid indicas, hybrids, exotics—everything was here. I convinced myself that this garden would fill half a *Cannabible* and immediately decided to find temporary lodging in the area so I could photograph the garden every few days.

   After my trembling and drooling became manageable, I started snapping photos. Most of the plants were over a month early, so I only snapped twenty or so shots, thinking I would photograph all of the individual plants as they matured throughout the next six weeks. After climbing out of the garden, we all laughed at the sight of my car still sitting parked with the door wide open from my absentminded exit. Then, I blissfully noticed that rubbing my body in any of a hundred different spots produced a unique aroma that hinted at what strain grazed that area. Eddy and his kind wife, Linda, invited me inside, and we began a smoking session that would have gotten a football stadium stoned.

Eddy's garden before the raid.

California outdoor organic.

Lepp making bubble hash, Eddy-style.

Eddy has a fascinating history with cannabis. For one thing, he was the first person arrested, tried, and acquitted under Proposition 215. He is also the national director for the American Medical Marijuana Association. He is an outspoken activist and freedom fighter, and a lover of all that is female. To make things even more interesting, he has been known to place full-page ads in the local newspaper saying, "Need a Doctor? I can help." Twice a month Eddy organizes for dozens of sick people to meet with a doctor who understands the benefits of medical marijuana. This has earned him a special place in the community, both in the eyes of the locals and the local law enforcement. Apparently it pissed off the feds.

After taking a few more photos of the main field from the house, my crew and I left to find a home base to work from for the next couple months.

A couple days later, I got the call. Eddy's Medicinal Garden had been raided by the DEA. Everyone was in jail, and all the plants were murdered and stolen.

One irie gardener had the un-irie misfortune of pulling up the driveway with three pounds of ganja on the passenger seat, while smoking a bong. As he parked and exhaled a massive cloud of

Does Marijuana Make You a Better Person?

BY JOAN BELLO

d o no harm? In our competitive culture, it is difficult to maintain personal conduct compatible with the higher ideals of love and compassion. Less self-absorption and more concern for the greater good, according to the psychology of transformation, can be accelerated: by practices of self-discipline, through personal reflection, through the administration of entheogens (substances that, when ingested, provide an experience of the divine), and at times by involuntary shocks to the system. These activities all share the common denominator of changing the invisible backdrop—known in esoteric language as the vibration. While conventional science does not recognize the vibratory essence or state of being of a person, there can be no question that life offers unlimited experiences of unique flavor, memory, and effect and that these nuances impact our whole being to determine perception and therefore behavior. In the ancient teaching of the Science of Vibration, to fine-tune one's own life energy purposefully and to blend it into a harmonious unity is descriptive of a more peaceful, less worried, more accepting and less distracted personality without hidden agendas and therefore naturally emanating concern for the greater good, born from love and compassion.

Throughout the records of all times and locales, there has always been a dominant culture with practical and self-serving doctrines and many who are counter to the culture, representative of the idealistic, whose interest is naturally, automatically, inherently turned toward inner reality and timeless values. One such explanation for the wide gap in individual human motivation was offered by the Fourth Way teacher Gurdjieff, who taught that only those persons with a "magnetic center" (mysterious inner elemental yearning) are attracted to the mystical or evolutionary experience. Eastern philosophy agrees that some souls in this embodiment are receptive to the ladder of evolution. Throughout the annals of recorded history all over the world, marijuana has served as a gentle, reliable, and sure way to open channels of awareness.

Marijuana has been a constant companion to those with spiritual leanings for thousands of years, having been most revered in the teachings of the Indian Vedas, where it was called "gift of the gods." It might just as appropriately have been called the "breath of life," since ultimately the marijuana experience is an enhancement and expansion of the breathing pattern from which the physical, psychological, and even the spiritual aspects of life are elevated. There are enormous benefits to the human organism garnered from the long-term regular utilization of marijuana, stemming directly from its innate, near-instantaneous effect of releasing tension in the pattern of the breath. According to Eastern philosophy, freedom and fullness of the entire breathing mechanism define well-being, and the patterns themselves affect our emotions and in turn our states of being. This is a mammoth topic in itself and volumes of Indian philosophy are taught concerning the wide-spectrum and deeply embedded extent that the "breath" holds over our consciousness.

Etymologically speaking, when we inspire, we take in spirit. The word *inspire* is derived from Latin *inspirare*, which means "to blow into," but the notion of a soul/spirit that enlivens as the force behind everything (especially underscored with each breath) is compartmentalized to weekly "worship." Predictably, the significance of inspiration has been lost. In holistic terms, to breathe is not limited to inhalation and exhalation of the lungs. It includes as well expansion and contraction of the thorax, motion of the chest, the abdomen, the interface of the organs, including nose, pharynx, larynx, trachea, bronchi, and associative nerves and blood vessels, as well as the individualized chemical responses to inspiration/expiration, and also the subtle energetic connection with mental processes. Breathing involves the whole being. Every cell breathes, and every breath defines the degree of affirmation of life that is being expressed by its unique vibration. Any tension in the breath, the body, or the mind is but a different dimension of the same problem, which affects chemical exchanges at the cellular level, which in turn exacerbates the constraint. On the other hand, a relaxed mind breathes with calm constancy and is experienced as body comfort.

It is the human tendency to repress what is unpleasant, accompanied and facilitated by constricting and diminishing breathing on a general and chronic basis, leading to increased and accumulated congestion over time. Usually, the older we become, the more rigid, conservative, intolerant, and anchored to our mores we likewise become. Unless we work against this natural entropic process, staleness accrues in our entire being. Marijuana is the great purifier. It expels the necrotic air in the bottom of our lungs while it disentangles the cobwebs in our intellects by lifting the habit of shallow breathing. When the breath is rhythmic and deepened by regular marijuana therapy, one can actually become sensitive enough to notice the moment when the muscles, the thoughts, and then the whole entity undergo inner relaxation, the result of restoring the natural electro-chemical balance by energizing/oxygenating/inspiring the organism.

Releasing the tension of years can be cathartic. It can also be traumatic to see clearly via the fully oxygenated brain what foolish notions and hostilities we may harbor; these moments of awareness can become contradictory and painful to our larger sense of ourselves and may disintegrate into what is called paranoia.

Of course, from a purely objective viewpoint, in the framework of holistic health, it is better not to build up the toxic staleness from the beginning. We can almost suggest that the wide extent of marijuana use by the younger generations all around the world signals choosing a healthy alternative of not becoming static in breath, body, or mind, as they have somehow intuited the freedom that accompanies fuller breath and how wonderfully marijuana assures it. This inherent ability of cannabis was described in the Ayurvedic texts of Indian wisdom, where *bhang* (marijuana) was prescribed as a general panacea for freedom from distress. Whereas many people cope with the insults of daily life and fear for personal survival by assuming a protective contraction around their bodies and their minds via diminished breathing, those who try to gain freedom of breath, however unconsciously, are unquestionably opting for health. To exhale stagnating air and to inhale deeply, rather than becoming angry and constricted in the face of frustration, marks the healthy personality. Untold millions of people find that marijuana melts their muscular armor, easily, safely, and almost immediately, making room for a breath of fresh air that literally wafts throughout the organism and allows for the exhaling of the energetic necrosis along with fear and frustration. Herein is what is meant by expanding the mind and raising the consciousness.

The uniqueness of this plant includes its molecular makeup, its uncanny conjoining with the human organism, its potential to cleanse the earth of its pollutants, its proven health benefits and medicinal features, and most of all, its incredible effect on human consciousness. Subjectively, the marijuana experience is one of being alert yet at ease. And all modern scientific measurements testify to the completely unique dualistic effects of this ancient and revered plant. In 1898, the majestic compilation of knowledge *Indian Hemps Drug Report* stated that cannabis has both sedative and stimulant effects simultaneously, which is the sought-after goal of yoga, meditation, spiritual disciplines, and holistic health. Because of its superior, simultaneously dualistic action, marijuana has the effect of balancing the inner workings of the organism, which results in higher functioning of the total organism in terms of health and serenity. Without psychosomatic distraction, with a quiet mind that can wrap itself around the creative, there is receptivity to the finer vibration within and without. This is a particular stance that is more than a state of body or a set in the mind, and approaches a feeling of well-being that smacks ever so slightly of magic. In this state, there is vibrational ripeness in the subject's consciousness in anticipation of awakening.

In premodern times, cannabis was utilized extensively as medicine and a sacrament because of its nearly immediate slowing and deepening of the breath automatically accompanied by a quieting of the incessant chatter of the mind and a harmonizing of the being. Until recently there was no scientific explanation of how it accomplishes such a profound benefit. Newer testing has demonstrated that most adults take in about $1/2$ liter of volume per breath, which is only one-sixth lung capacity. When marijuana is administered, the general intake of a full breath rises to nearly six liters, an almost twelvefold increase in delivery to the entire being. Little wonder that physiological distress of every kind is wondrously alleviated and that awareness and sensitivity on all levels are gloriously heightened. Whenever the blood oxygen levels change, however slightly, a chain reaction through all processing occurs, including the mental. Marijuana's subtle effect on the breath is experienced as a gentle almost unnoticeable deep sigh of relief, which quickly results in an easy pattern of breathing and coalesces into biochemical balance. This interface takes place between the electromagnetic charge of the many types of marijuana compounds and the prehistoric receptor system that is in and throughout all the cells of our bodies, seemingly tailor-made to respond to the vibratory charge of cannabis. The extensive receptor network is responsible for toning, regulating, and smoothing almost all activities that sustain life. This receptor system was uncovered during experiments trying to understand the effects of marijuana. Natural body chemicals were later discovered that interface with the cannabinoid system, and these compounds were fittingly named *ananda*—the Indian word for "bliss"—in recognition that anandamides are the bliss givers of human experience, called the good mood consciousness by the very conservative Institute of Medicine when it described the general effect of marijuana.

The physical-psychological harmony that accrues from marijuana therapy can really never be fully appreciated from the objective viewpoint, since the subjective experience far exceeds the proven benefits of balance to health. With the administration of marijuana, brain wave synchronization is achieved, digestive ease accomplished, blood pressure stabilized, dysfunction in breathing patterns reversed, chronic pain diminished, pain thresholds raised, appetite stimulated, temperature regulated, and muscular problems relaxed. From the emotional vantage point, the inner experience of a free and easy breath is the signature of nonworry. Deep and regular breathing expresses trust, not fear. Silent and slow inspiration and exhalation are the signposts of calm and kindness.

A relaxed and well-oxygenated body allows the individual to experience a calmer and less-identified mind-set. By changing the vibration of self-worry, marijuana therapy heightens awareness. The vibration is raised. Over the course of time, this more aware state of higher consciousness becomes habitual. Once the doors to perception have been opened, we have been warned, they do not close again. From all the science and the esoteric philosophy, as well as from my own long-term association with marijuana, a less restricted, more relaxed, and more fully oxygenated body allows for a mental serenity that could not be the case if the body were at a lower vibration. The entire goal of esoteric philosophy is to raise awareness. It is taught that all acts of unkindness, every negative thought, are but the result of the human state of having forgotten/lost the true reality. All methods of practice are therefore toward the one goal of awakening to this beneficent reality. In that, cannabis can play a major role.

The Cannabible is a glorious tribute to cannabis perfection in all its diversity. The incredible array of differing strains reminds us of the subtle and superior possible vibrations in consciousness sadly missing in the lives of most marijuana lovers. The majority of us must make do with the less potent mass-produced quality of herb. But Jason King has brought us poignantly close to the reality in his extreme photography. The vibrancy of the specimens that ooze from these pages is the supreme grade needed for the successful lifelong experience of marijuana therapy.

Gallery

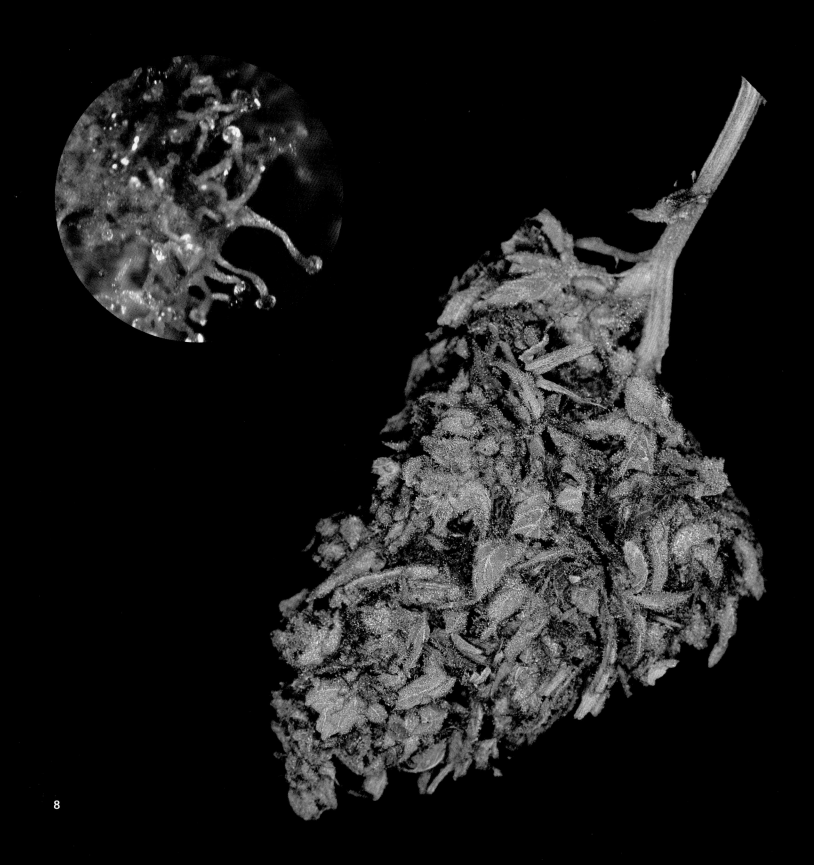

8

Afghooey

Afghooey is a mostly indica strain that is gaining popularity in California connoisseur circles. She was created by crossing a Maui Haze with the original Afghani #1, which she very much leans toward. Afghooey is indeed a very gooey plant, and a large producer as well. She is above average in potency; however, the narcotic high produced is not my personal favorite. The flavor is light and woody, almost nutty, yet not as strong as I would like it to be. This sample was grown indoors organically in soil.

AK47 X Kong

This herb smells like old Nepali sativa hash with hints of bubblegum. The flavor is similar, but with an added bark tone. The breeders must have used a very nice **AK47** phenotype for the father. The mother, **Kong,** is reportedly an unstable clone bought by Laughing Moon Seed Company for $40,000 and is said to be the largest yielder ever. This claim has never panned out. Nevertheless, this bud was in fact extremely dank.

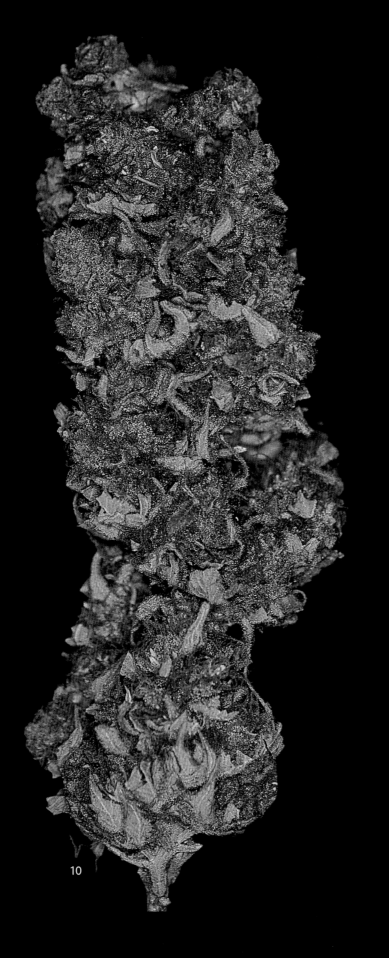

Akala

Nebu, a breeder from the Pacific Northwest, is the creator of this fine four-way hybrid. The father is a California indica X Hawaiian sativa, and the mother is a Northern Lights X Blueberry. It has a grapey Thai flavor, with sappy butter toffee undertones. The high produced was instantaneous, and quite impressive. Nebu grows these ladies using the "vegan" organic method, meaning no animal products of any kind were used. These karma-free nuggets were cured in cedar boxes, and some were over two years old. Given ideal curing conditions, they seemed to be only getting better.

Higher Organics

BY NEBU

Organic agriculture may be defined as an ecological production management system that promotes and enhances biodiversity, biological cycles, and soil biological activity. In conventional agriculture, synthetic fertilizers, pesticides, and herbicides, growth regulators, antibiotics, and hormone stimulators and the inhumane treatment of animals are commonly employed. These techniques frequently lead to adverse, often irreversible, effects upon the environment. Cannabis cultivators may not have as much impact upon the environment as a typical agricultural farmer, but those who are conscientious, and also prefer the healthiest and best-tasting product, can use organic guidelines to have an even smaller impact upon the earth.

The underlying principle of organic agriculture is to produce optimum quality and quantity using methods that restore, maintain, and enhance ecological harmony. However, the current guidelines typically include industrial agricultural waste and by-products like bone and blood meal, emulsions, and manures, as well as a subset of "acceptable" synthetics such as copper oxides and sulfates, hydrogen peroxide, potassium bicarbonate, streptomycin, tetracycline, ethylene, lignin sulfonate, etc. These guidelines vary by country, region, and even state, with various private certification systems and government agencies stepping in (likely diluting the whole concept further).

Genetically modified organisms (GMOs) and amendments are another gray area of yet unknown consequences and serious concern. Taking the principles of organics to heart requires scrutiny of these guidelines. It requires higher organics. Many options for fertilization and disease and pest control are available to the higher organic cannabis cultivator. For those few who have close relations with organic farmers, domestic animal by-products such as bone meal and manure may still be viable options.

Another option is wild-crafted organics, utilizing guano from wild birds and bats as a fertilizer source. Wild-crafted cannabis organics relies primarily on guano. Native Americans recognized the beneficial properties of guano over a thousand years ago. This guano may be mixed directly in the growing medium, applied as a top coat, or composted in teas and used in foliar feeding and hydro-organics. Creating compost teas from guano provides for an even greater beneficial microorganism content. In addition to being an excellent fertilizer, guano teas are also beneficial foliars in disease prevention, as any pathogenic organisms that may land on the leaf surface must compete with the beneficial organisms and have a greatly reduced chance to infect the plants.

A third growing option, vegan organics, eliminates animal products altogether. Before the symbiotic relationship between plants and animals evolved, plants survived without animals, and so can your cannabis. Alfalfa, kelp, soybean meal, nettles, cottonseed meal, comfrey, soft rock phosphate, greensand, and montmorillonite clay (all organic, non-GMO) are just some of the options available to meet nutrient, mineral, and trace element requirements.

Plant extracts and biological controls are some options available for pest and disease control and prevention. It is beyond the scope of this section to share all the concerns with nonorganic and traditional organic gardening techniques, or to detail all the components and methodologies used in higher organics. It is, however, this author's hope that the preceding will inspire some to pause, reflect, further research, inspect, and possibly put into effect some of the concepts outlined. The potential impact could be far-reaching or, conversely, too close to home. After all, who will guarantee that sack of commercially produced steamed bone meal does not contain mad cow disease or some other lethal infectious agent?

Apollo 11

This much-loved Brothers Grimm strain could be no less than fantastic when you consider its lineage. The mother plant was a lemony Genius (see page 67) and the father plant a Cinderella 99 (see page 36). This hybrid leans toward the sativa side and produces a very up and happy high—great for a long walk on the beach. The flavor is wonderful as well, although completely different from the aroma. The nose is slightly mentholated, and a bud lets off a mild astringent aroma when gently squeezed. When smoked, it's like peppery green apple, even star fruit. The exhale is tropical fruity, yet peppery. Yum.

Interesting note: These plants were grown legally for medicine in a registered garden in Oregon. One day, the police showed up, and a polite officer asked this grower if he could show the crop to the young officer that he was training, to make it easier for him to identify marijuana in the future. The grower grudgingly agreed, and when the cops checked the garden, there were a few more plants than allowed in the grow room. The cop informed the grower that he must take the extra plants, but he actually let the grower pick which plants he wanted to keep. This was one of the keepers.

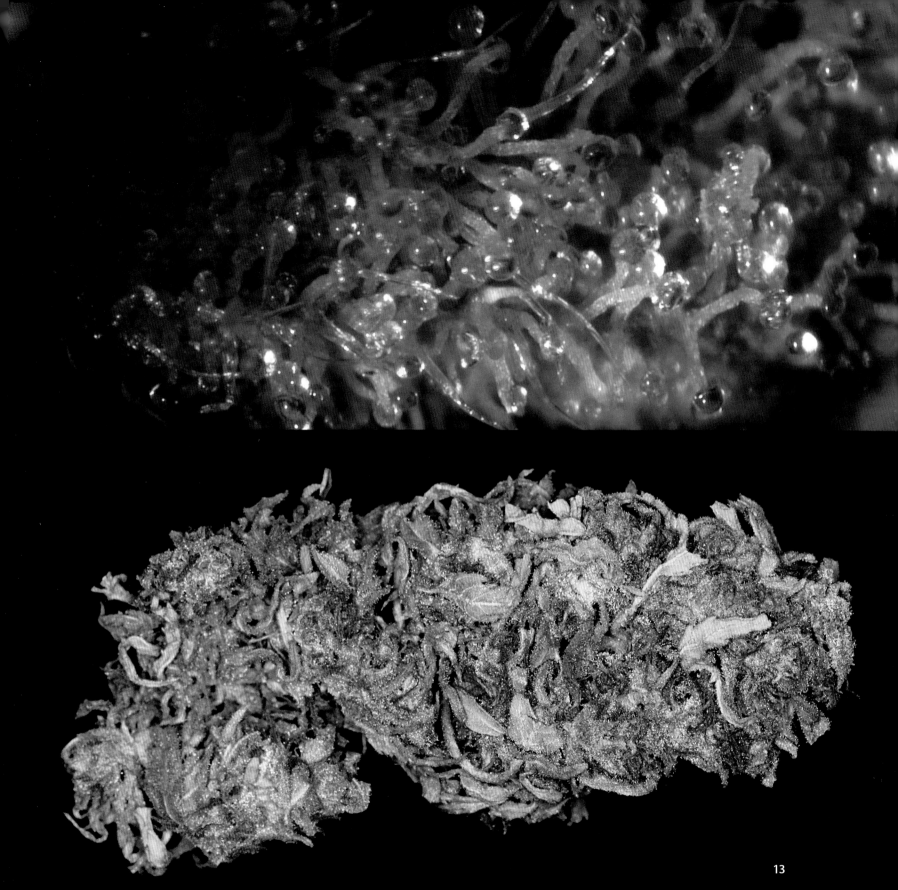

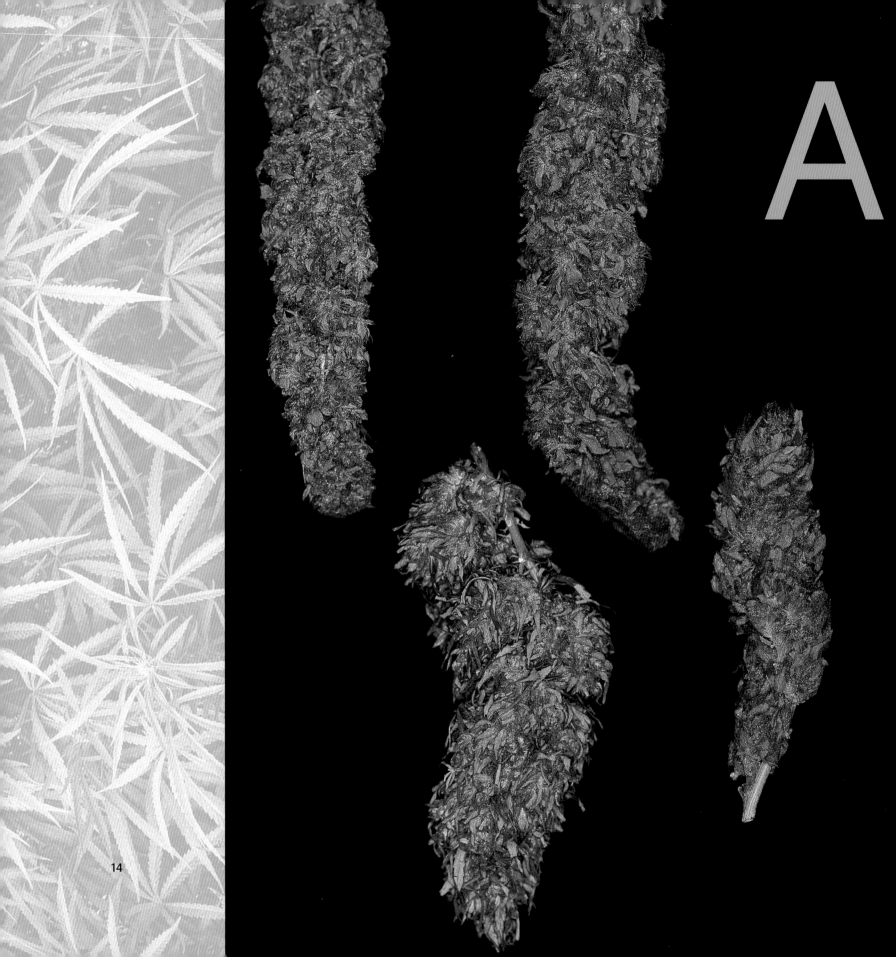

14

A

ustralia

Australian Cannabis Cup

For the lucky forty or so people with the special pass, the Australian Cannabis Cup was a night to be remembered, despite alleged claims of memory loss. On the last night of Mardi Grass, we were shuttled to an unnamed location and led to a beautiful country house that contained a large table with phat colas of about thirty strains of spectacular Aussie grown ganja. Most were outdoor grown, or "bush," as the locals call it, but there were outstanding indoor samples as well. No one was allowed to touch the buds, which was a major bummer for me, because I would have to touch and move them to set up a tripod, in order to properly photograph them. After pleading with the drooling crowd and showing them the first volume of *The Cannabible*, in an offer of respect to the cultivators, I was given five minutes to photograph (and touch!) the entire load. Well, I did the best I could. I was surprised and a little disappointed to learn that an indoor sample won the cup. Yes, it was a lovely Bubblegum X Blueberry cross, and it was delectable without doubt, but some of the outdoor sappy, man-goey sativas were much more desirable in my opinion. Either way, I am proud to say that I sampled every one and was very impressed with Australian ganja. These people take their herb very seriously.

Mr. Nice and Hybrids

Here we have **Mr. Nice** and three hybrids, all photographed in Australia (Mr. Nice X Blueberry, Mr. Nice X Mango, and Mr. Nice X Thai). Mr. Nice is a strain named after Howard Marks, possibly the largest cannabis smuggler in history. The lineage of Mr. Nice, a Sensi Seeds strain, is as follows: G13 X Hash Plant. Here Mr. Nice, a double indica, is crossed with three different tropical sativas, producing extremely vigorous hybrids of exceptional quality.

Mr. Nice X Blueberry
(hydro)

Mr. Nice X Mango
(hydro)

Mr. Nice
(hydro)

Mr. Nice X Thai
(outdoor)

17

Monster-size Aussie Haze plant

19

Mullumbimby Madness

One of the more famous Australian strains, the **Madness** was created in a similar fashion to the original Haze. Imported sativa strains were bred into the mix every year for several years, combining genetics from Thailand, Colombia, Mexico, Hawaii, New Guinea, India, and Lebanon. As the surfers and hippies brought in new strains each year, the best of them were bred into the Madness. The result is a super sativa with massive size and potent, spicy smoke. These plants were photographed in the bush in Australia, mate!

This bud is about as trippy as it gets. **Nevilles Haze** is almost pure Haze, with a touch of Northern Lights. Although this bud takes forever to finish (over fourteen weeks), the resulting herb is of phenomenal sativa quality. The high is profoundly weird, definitely not for lightweights. It could easily be considered psychedelic. The flavor has pronounced earthy and spicy notes, delicious to say the least. This batch was grown organically outdoors in eastern Australia.

Nevilles Haze

Mardi Grass

Deep Down Under, in a little alternative village known as Nimbin, there is a raging cannabis celebration that happens each year in the beginning of May. The name of this event is Mardi Grass, and serious cannabis enthusiasts owe it to themselves to attend one of these fantastic parties. And while Mardi Grass certainly is an amazing party, with music, food, dance, laughter, and most importantly, an abundance of gooey kind bud, it doesn't stop there. Mardi Grass is also a drug law reform rally of amazing proportions, with diverse speakers making their passionate plea to the masses for sane drug laws. This peaceful village simply refuses to accept the drug war, and they do it with an Aussie style that is clever, passionate, and quite endearing.

The entire event is organized by volunteers, and a tremendous amount of work it is. But year after year, since '93, they pull it off gloriously. There is nonstop entertainment, with plenty of classic events, such as the Hemp Olympix, which includes such challenging events as the Growers Ironperson, Bong Toss and Yell, and a joint-rolling contest. Then there is the Kombi Caravan, an endless parading caravan of decked-out Volkswagen buses (they call them Kombis down under). There is also unorganized fun everywhere, with musicians and DJs popping up in any imaginable spot to seduce your ears and get your butt moving.

In short, if you like to party, want to check out an awesome new country, and have been less than impressed with the Cannabis Cup in Amsterdam, I highly recommend checking out Mardi Grass. Them Aussies really know how to party! For more information, check out their website: www.nimbinmardigrass.com.

Powdery Mildew

While bud hunting on the West Coast, I come across garden after garden infested with a nasty disease known as powdery mildew. It seems to be hitting almost every grower, both indoor and out. Many theorized that it was a government-created fungus designed to attack and destroy local ganja crops, but I do not agree. Powdery mildew is seriously threatening Northern California's multimillion-dollar wine grape crop also, as well as countless other crops. Luckily, there is an organic cure for powdery mildew, though I was surprised to learn that most ganja growers do not know of it and suffer massive losses every year as a result. The cure is called AQ10, and it comes from Ecogen, Inc. The key with this stuff is that it must be applied as soon as there are any signs of powdery mildew. If caught and treated at this early stage, the mildew should pose no serious threat. I can't stress enough the importance of not smoking mold or mildew. Yuck!

For information on AQ10, contact Ecogen:
Ecogen, Inc.
2005 Cabot Boulevard West
P.O. Box 3023
Langhorne, Pennsylvania 19047-3023
215-757-1590
Fax: 215-757-2956

Bionic Blueberry X Grapefruit

This is a hybrid cross of two wonderfully fruity strains. **Bionic Blueberry** (not to be confused with DJ Short's Blueberry) was the male, and **Grapefruit,** a relatively old clone from the Pacific Northwest, was the female. There is a pronounced grapefruit flavor in there, with spicy and fragrant undertones. Nebu takes the credit for this one, and she, like all of Nebu's plants, is vegan, grown organically and indoors in soil.

Hydro

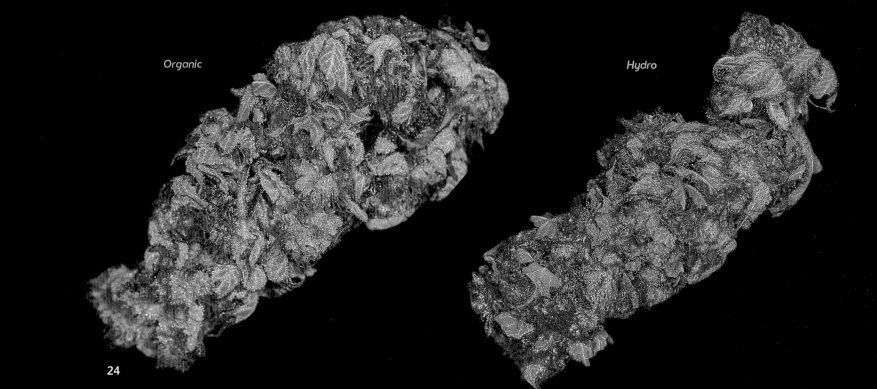

Organic

Hydro

24

Black Domina

This superpotent indica is an offering from Sensi Seeds. A California outdoor version of **Black Domina** was featured in the first volume of *The Cannabible*. Here we have two different indoor versions, one grown organically in soil and one grown hydroponically. All had the same noticeable greasy hash oil flavor, but the outdoor was the smoothest and most enjoyable smoke. This stuff is extremely strong, even narcotic—the kind of herb that can immediately end your day.

Black Russian

By crossing his unique Blackberry plant (see page 29) with a cherry liqueur phenotype of AK47, Nebu created **Black Russian.** The flavor of this vegan and organically grown bud is like black cherries, with elegant notes of cacao. Truly a dessert herb, and not lacking potency at all, Black Russian was extremely satisfying in every way.

25

Water Hash

A hash phenomenon is sweeping the planet right now, allowing just about anyone to make the finest hash imaginable from trim, using only some specialized bags, a mixer, ice, a bucket, and water. This technique operates on the principle that resin glands are heavier than water, and are also insoluble in water. Special bags, whose bottoms are made of screens with mesh sizes that approach those of resin glands, are placed in a bucket. The top bag is then filled with trim or small buds (usually), and ice and water. The colder the water the better, as the resin glands are more rigid when cold and therefore break free from the leaf material more easily. This concoction is mixed for fifteen minutes and then left to sit for thirty minutes. As the mixture sits, the magic of gravity takes effect, as the vegetative matter and debris rise and the resin glands sink. At this point, the bags are simply lifted out one at a time. The first bag removes the mass of leaves and ice. The second bag contains anything too big to be a resin gland—debris. This is discarded. The remaining bags contain resin glands sorted according to size. These are collected and immediately dried, to prevent the possibility of mold setting in. And each of the different size bags produces hash with noticeably different highs! This is one of the many areas in which marijuana appreciation leaves wine appreciation in the dust. Considering that (in comparison to the hash that was available in the 1970s) virtually all imported hash is now low quality, this

process is a God-send to hash-lovers around the world. (And many who never even know what a hash-lover they were!)

The water hash technique started in the early 1980s with Sadu Sam, who ran a series of ads in *High Times* magazine for his amazing water-based hash-making system. In his literature, he thanks Neville the King of Cannabis Castle for discovering this technique. Legend has it that an unnamed American gave the idea to Neville. This system was very crude and simple, yet it could actually produce fine-quality hashish. Basically, some buds would be ground through a strainer and placed in a jar, which was then nearly filled with water. This jar would then be sealed and vigorously shaken for a few minutes, and then left to settle. After five to ten minutes, the floating debris would be skimmed off and placed in another jar for a second run. The resin glands that sunk to the bottom of these jars would be poured into a coffee filter, which was then folded and squeezed inside a T-shirt for quick removal of most of the remaining water. (How bad could it turn out when you start with buds!)

The first automated machine was built by a man called Baba Bob. It was a large 12-inch PVC pipe with different size screens placed across the pipe, with the largest holes first, and so on down the pipe. The device was placed under a tap of cold water. This device was only used a few times and wasn't shown to many people, but it did exist.

The first water hash machine that was sold to the public was called The Extractor. Designed in the U.S., but manufactured in Yugoslavia, it was poorly constructed, cumbersome to use, and quite expensive. One day while brainstorming on how to economize The Extractor, Mila Jansen, the hash genius from Amsterdam who owns the Pollinator Company (www.pollinator.nl) decided that there needed to be a screen halfway down the bucket. A man named Eldon then suggested the use of a bag. Mila sewed and experimented with many different screens and after six weeks, a second bag was added. This system makes hash so pure that it bubbles and sizzles when smoked, and packs a potency that's almost frightening. The only thing stronger is butane-extraction hash, which is not natural and leaves undesirable chemical residues. All this could be created from the trim that many growers normally disposed of after manicuring their buds! Mila and friends experimented with kits of up to six bags, but in their research, they found that the smaller glands contained a higher percentage of cellulose, and therefore less THC. They decided that for ultimate quality, a two-bag kit made the most sense. Mila then manufactured and marketed this system as the Ice-o-Lator.

At this point, an enterprising man calling himself Bubble Man (www.freshheadies.com) entered the scene, manufacturing and heavily promoting six- and seven-bag kits in five- or twenty-gallon sizes, with each bag utilizing a screen with a different size mesh. The first two bags can remove the trim and contaminants, and the last five bags contain all the precious resin glands, sorted according to specific size. Bubble Man is not kidding when he says, "If it don't bubble, it ain't worth the trouble!" After smoking some wicked full-melt bubble for a while, you won't want to smoke anything else.

Full melt bubble at 75x.

Lifting all of those heavy water-filled bags repeatedly can get quite strenuous on the back. I've known people to hurt themselves. The twenty-gallon kit is asking for a hernia, even with someone to help. The next advancement of water-hash technology will have three major benefits: 1) No heavy lifting; 2) Any amount can be made in one large batch; and 3) Increased quality. Luckily, this advancement can be used with existing kits. Check www.thecannabible.com to keep up with the latest developments.

One interesting and attractive possibility with the bag systems involves traveling to countries where large quantities of (usually low quality) ganja can be obtained very cheap and processing it into super-high-quality hash. One could theoretically go to a Third World country and purchase a pound of ganja for anywhere from $5 to about $100. This pound could then easily be made into an ounce or so of full-melt, mind-numbing water hash that is much more enjoyable to smoke then any amount of (low-grade) ganja.

One reason that water hash is special is because you know it is not contaminated. Most of the world's imported hash is cut with things that would scare you—lard, tallow, wax, sheep's fat, cow dung, petroleum products, and so forth. Another benefit of smoking water hash is the harm reduction theory. The hash is so incredibly potent that you simply cannot smoke too much of it. A heavy marijuana smoker, who smokes say seven grams a day, would have a hard time smoking one and a half grams of super-pure water hash in a day. Less smoke equals less carcinogens equals a healthier high.

Black Widow

We saw the indoor **Black Widow** in the first volume of *The Cannabible*. Here we have an outdoor-grown California version, and it is far superior to the indoor version. This was easily the most astringent bud I've ever smoked, and to be honest, it's almost too much. A nug broken up reeks like paint thinner or turpentine, and the thick, greasy smoke is a bit much for some. Personally, I wouldn't want to smoke it every day, but once in a while, it makes a nice and unique treat. This strain does not resemble White Widow in any way. Does anybody know of this strain's lineage? I sure don't! Note: This is not the same Black Widow sold by Mr. Nice Seed Company.

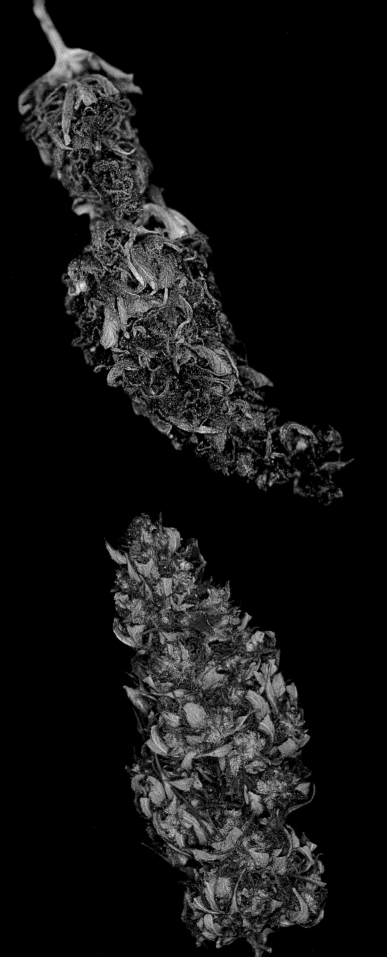

Blackberry

This deliciously unique strain is another offering from Nebu Organiques. Coming from a seed pulled out of a freaky mystery bud scored in Northern California, this strain was developed by Nebu to its current state. It possesses many unique flavors rarely experienced in today's marijuana, including geranium, opium, menthol, astringent, and sweet and sour—interestingly, all high notes. This is easily some of the most unique herb I've ever seen. The potency is mild, making **Blackberry** a good daytime bud.

Also shown is a Blackberry bud from Mullaway Seeds in Australia (bottom left). These blokes really know their herb. Not surprisingly, they often win the Nimbin Cannabis Cup. This outdoor grown nugget, which seems unrelated to Nebu's Blackberry, was fantastic all around. Sweet, tangy, and with mouthwatering berry tones, I felt grateful to receive it as a gift. The high had a slightly euphoric tinge that made everything more enjoyable. I saw and photographed about twenty strains from Mullaway and was extremely impressed with their diverse collection. They have some unique and wonderful strains, which I look forward to seeing more of.

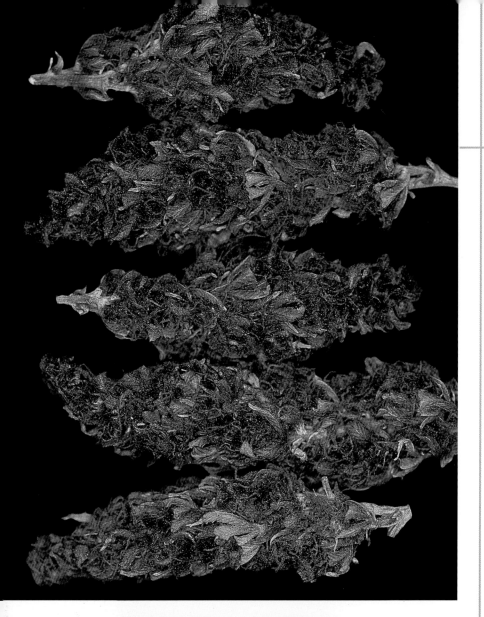

Blackberry

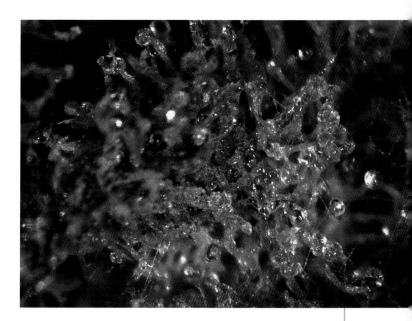

Webbing left behind from spider-mites.

This lovely Northern California indica strain has a sweet cinnamon flavor, all at once flowery and tangy, with hints of Provençal herbs. She was grown outdoors organically, right next to a house, and received all the attention and love possible. The high is thick and heady, a warm buzz emanating from the center of my brain, pulsating out to my toes and beyond.

Blue Confusion

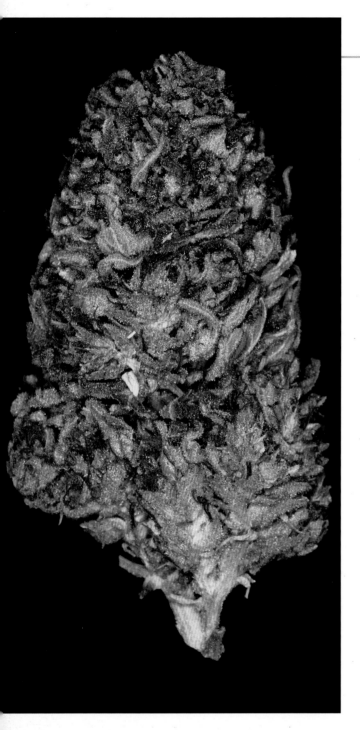

Blue Moon

Tangy and pungent, **Blue Moon** is a clone from the Shelter Cove area of Humboldt, California. She currently exists only in female form and, when broken apart, has a tangy and pungent solventlike odor not unlike Pledge furniture polish. As for the effects, Blue Moon produces a high that is very satisfying and sedative. This is great herb for unwinding after a long day. This sample was grown outdoors organically in Mendocino, California.

Blue Widow Hyrbids

Here we have a couple of strains crossed with **Blue Widow,** a lovely **hybrid** consisting of Blueberry and a '98 Aloha White Widow. The taste of this herb closely resembles that of blue cotton candy, and it made my mouth water, literally. Personally, I liked it more than any other Widow cross that I've tried. The fact that it was grown outdoors (mostly) organically in California definitely helped (as opposed to hydro-grown Amsterdam bud).

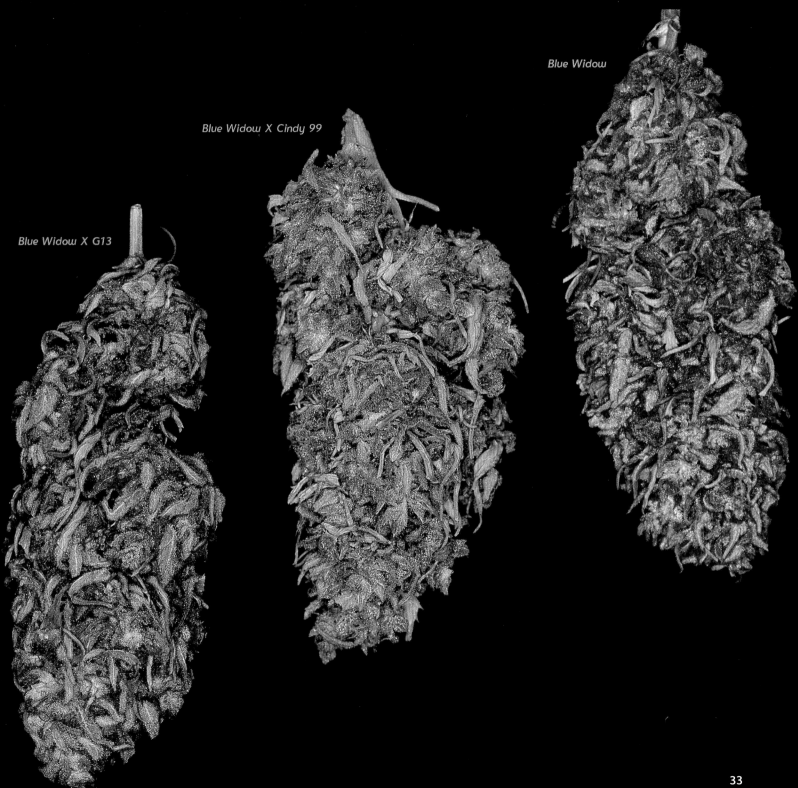

Blue Widow X G13

Blue Widow X Cindy 99

Blue Widow

33

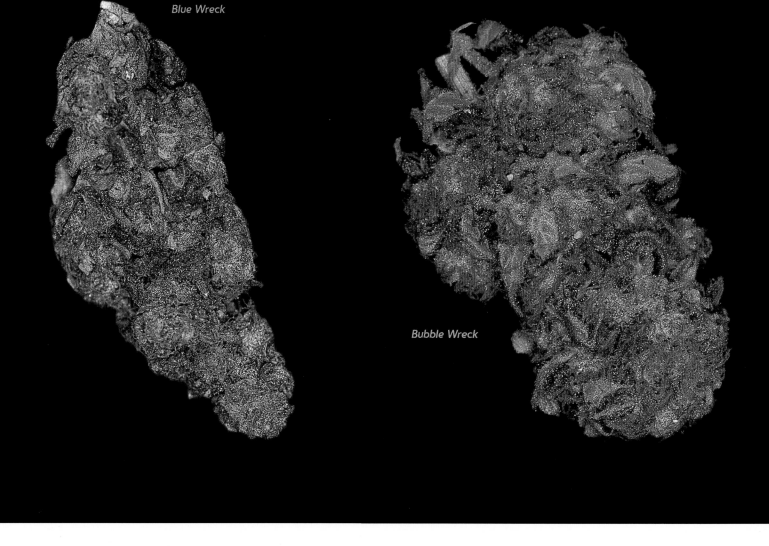

Blue Wreck

Bubble Wreck

Blue Wreck and Bubble Wreck

This goopy bud is a cross of DJ Short's Blueberry (see the first volume of *The Cannabible*) and Trainwreck (see page 165–68) and was grown organically indoors in soil. Grown by a woman, it reminded me that women grow the best herb. Think about it—it *is* a female plant. This bud had a multitude of luscious fruity flavors, ranging from blueberry to citrus, and the high was no less impressive. The high is soaring and floaty, yet functional, perfect for a midafternoon fatty.

Also shown is **Bubble Wreck,** predictably a Bubblegum X Trainwreck hybrid. You can't go wrong with parents like these. It was grown organically indoors in soil, in an Octagon growing system.

Cannabis and Chocolate

At long last, science has finally answered the age-old question: why do we crave chocolate when we're high? Scientists from the Neurosciences Institute in La Jolla, California, have discovered that anandamide (from the Sanskrit word *ananda*, which means "bliss" or "ecstasy"), an organic chemical that is present in the human brain, is also present in chocolate (although in highly varied amounts, depending on brand). Anandamide, so it seems, is highly euphoric (at least some lucky lab animals seem to think it is). But even more interesting, the scientists subsequently discovered two additional cannabinoids that naturally occur in chocolate. These newly discovered "noids" dramatically slowed down the breakdown of anandamide in laboratory tests. Translation: chocolate can prolong your high (and maybe even intensify it too!). If nothing else, it tastes freakin' fantastic.

I recommend a vegan, organic, dark chocolate, with no white (refined) sugar. Find a chocolate that uses evaporated cane juice instead, available from any good health food store. It's no huge secret that chocolate is not very good for you, but you can minimize the damage by eating "clean" chocolates like these. White sugar and dairy are much worse for your health than the actual cacao itself.

If you would like to learn more about chocolate, I highly recommend reading *The New Taste of Chocolate*, by Maricel E. Presilla, also from Ten Speed Press. This book is The ChocoBible as far as I'm concerned, with lavish photographs of dozens of strains of cacao, as well as the actual beans. I was fascinated to learn how similar cacao and cannabis are in their history, breeding, diversity, threats, and so forth.

Choco-covered bud, anyone?

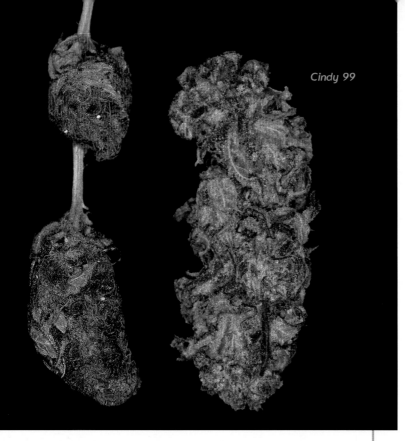
Cindy 99

Builder

This over-twenty-five-year-old exotic sativa strain was photographed in Humboldt, California. Visually stunning, unfortunately she was grown with chemicals in a hydroponic setup, and suffered greatly as a result. Even though it was properly flushed, the smoke still bit me in the throat and had a noticeable chemical flavor. Just as the human immune system, and even our gene pool, are being weakened by all the chemicals we are exposed to in daily life, so are plants weakened by living on chemicals. Having heard what I had to say, this intelligent and conscientious grower agreed to give organics a try, so look for organic **Builder** in *The Cannabible 3*.

Blueberry X Cindy 99

Hopefully, by now, everybody knows and loves DJ Short's **Blueberry.** A Canadian Blueberry was crossed with a special, extremely berryish DJ Short Blueberry in 1999 for the male side of this hybrid. Brothers Grimm are the creators of **Cindy 99** (at right), a freaky, fruity, and hazy ganja strain that is much adored by the lucky ones that have access to her. Cindy was the female. A cross of such fantastic strains could be no less than excellent. This stunning hybrid, grown outdoors in Northern California, has a thick, tangy, fruity flavor that lingers on the taste buds just about forever. She holds her flavors when so many others have given up. The high is extremely powerful, a blissful experience that was all at once euphoric and mind-expanding.

Bullrider

Bullrider

Here we have a hydroponically grown sample of **Bullrider,** a popular California strain that was featured organic-style in the first volume of *The Cannabible.* Frankly and predictably, I like the organic one better. The breeder contacted me with some details about the name—apparently, it gets you so high that you feel like you've ridden a bull.

Also shown is **BullNana,** a cross of Bullrider and Bwanana, a Sweet Skunk X Maui Haze cross. This nug was grown outdoors organically in Northern California and has a strong herbal flavor with affy tones of hashiness, and a floaty dreamy high.

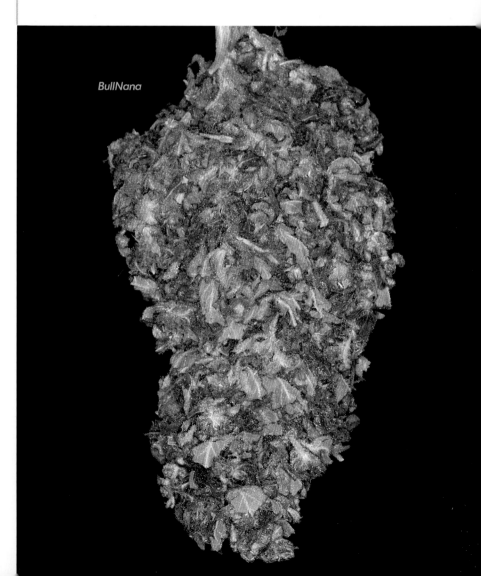

BullNana

California Outdoor Organic

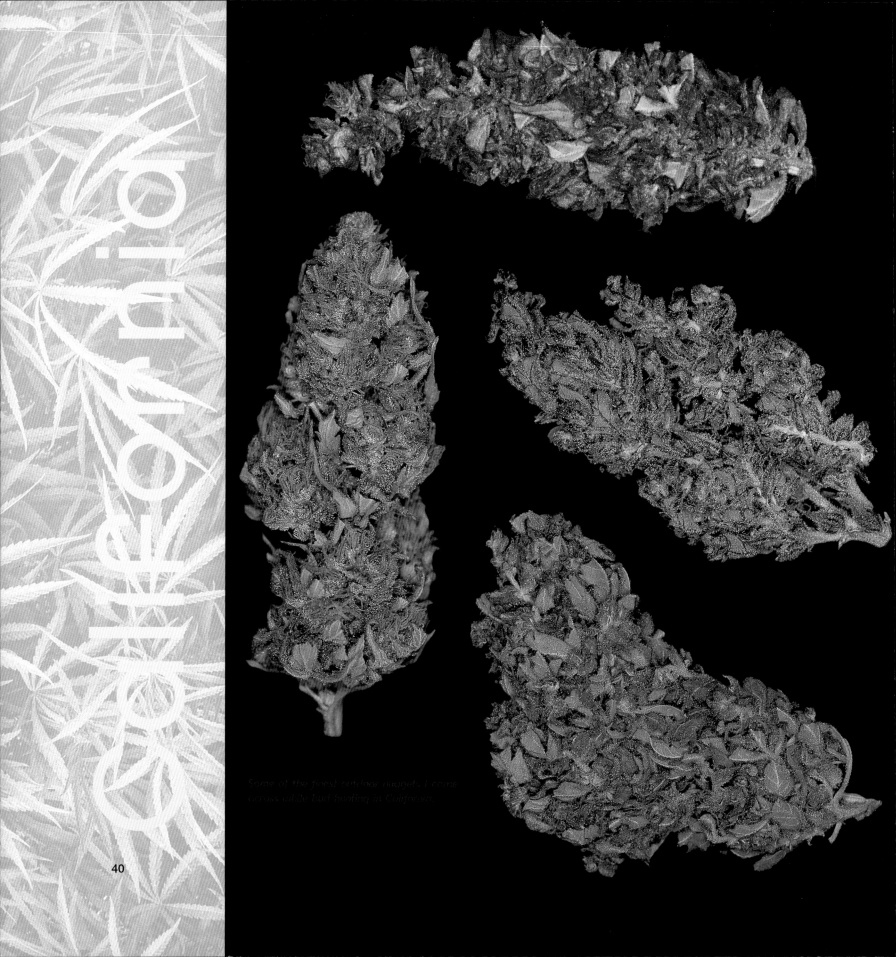

Some of the finest outdoor nugget I came across while bud hunting in California.

ganic

43

44

Cali Orange

Cali Orange is a California-bred clone from 1980 and is not to be confused with the Sensi Seeds version. She balances out at 50 percent indica and 50 percent sativa and has a creamy orange aroma that is simply delectable. Luckily, she tastes as good as she smells—orange cream soda flavors dance on the taste buds, almost guaranteed to produce a big smile on any toker's face. This delicious strain produces a clearheaded working high and is definitely worth adding to the collection of any breeding program. It has a sixty-six-day flowering time.

Cambodian

This hefty sativa cola was grown outdoors in California, although the strain is originally from Cambodia. The flavor is earthy, musty, and robust, and reminded me of good Thai bud from the old days. Thailand's close proximity to Cambodia probably has something to do with this. The high from this bud was extremely clear and functional, even subtle compared to most of today's indica-dominated strains. I look forward to visiting Cambodia some day to photograph the local strains in their native environment.

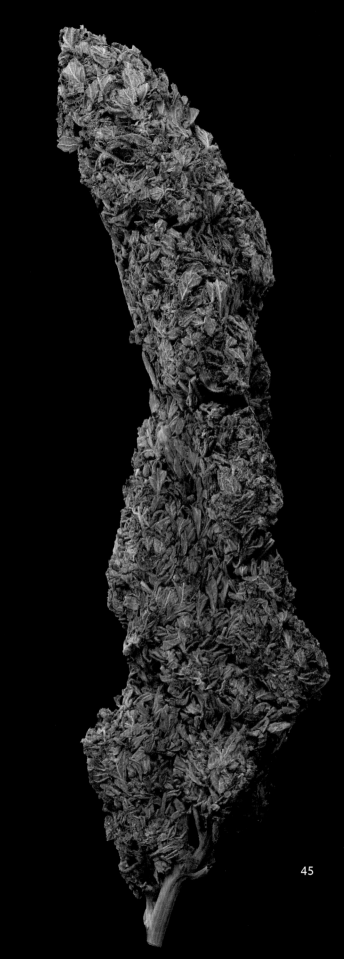

45

There is an interesting story about **"the Chem."**
Apparently, she was a much-adored strain in the
Colorado area for years, but for some strange reason, her best qualities were only apparent when
grown with chemicals. Despite many efforts with
organics, to get the Chem to produce connoisseur-
grade herb pretty much required that massive
doses of chemicals be applied. So, in honor of this,
the strain was named "Chem." Now, I am a huge
believer in organic buds (and organic everything
else too!), but I must admit, the Chem is phenomenal. And yes, it is better than the organic version
(see the Dawg, page 52). This is the only time I
have ever experienced chemically grown buds being
better in any way than organically grown buds.
Luckily, the grower of this hydro Chem was an
expert, and the plants were properly flushed before
harvest. Two bong hits of this powerful smoke had
my head throbbing and beads of sweat forming on
my brow. The flavor is incredible—it's this disgust-
ingly good, sappy, candied thing, electric, tangy,
petrol bliss. Seems that it could possibly be related
to Diesel. Highly recommended for hydro growers if
you can get it.

Chem

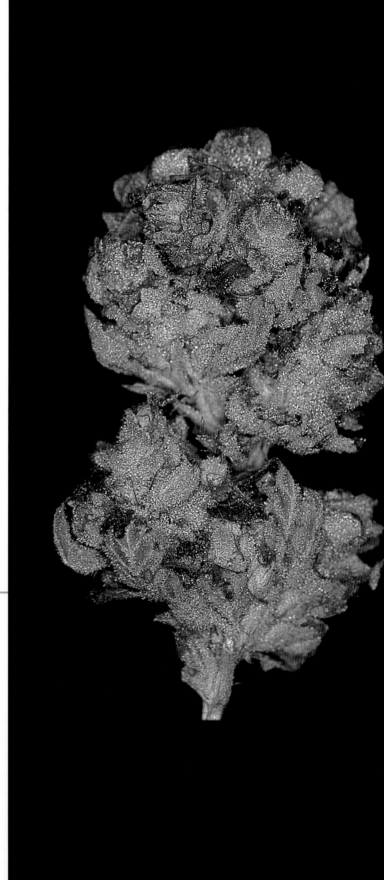

Coastal Gold

Coming from the Sonoma coast of California, this golden ganja was grown organically outdoors. Mostly a sativa, this old-school Cali strain probably has origins in Colombia or Mexico. Though the flavor isn't particularly strong, it is deeply earthy, rich, and satisfying. The high was mild and pleasant in all ways, with a smooth return to reality. It's nice to see some growers resisting all the new "designer" strains and sticking with old proven strains, thus keeping them in circulation. This is crucially important these days, as the homogenization of today's cannabis strains threatens the future of the kind.

Coral Reef

Here we have one of my personal favorites, **Coral Reef**. Her origins are a mystery for now, but this strain has a flavor that I've never before experienced in ganja, or anywhere else for that matter. Words simply cannot describe the flavor, but here is my stoned attempt. It's a cool cardamom, lemon zest thing, and it is extreme! It has as much flavor as any other strain out there, even HP13, yet it is completely different. The high is outstanding as well, a warm and tingling buzz felt from the top of the head to all the extremities, and a major jolt to the creativity circuitry of the brain. This plant grows with stunning purple outlines on the inner leaf surfaces. Clones are now available at Northern California Cannabis Buyer Clubs.

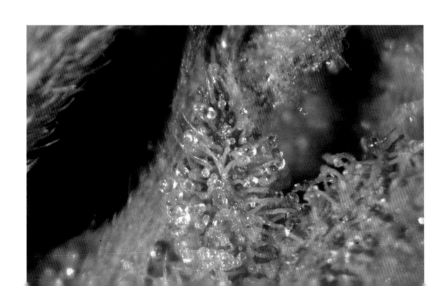

On Judging Cannabis

Something important to consider when judging a cannabis strain is that you are more likely judging the grower and growing conditions as well as the individual seed, rather than the strain itself. Remember, the relationship of seeds to one another is much like comparing siblings in your family. Even though two children have the same parents, the children are completely different. So, if you try a strain and are not impressed, this doesn't necessarily mean that the strain is unimpressive. It could just be a "weak sister." (Note: When clones are used, this is not the case, for clones have the same genetic makeup as the parent from which they were taken.) Alternatively, you could be judging a novice grower's crop or even the product of a poorly ventilated grow-room, for example. In writing *The Cannabibles*, I have done my best to judge the actual strains themselves, not the grower or growing conditions. I achieved this by, whenever possible, viewing and sampling several different batches of a given strain, each grown by a different person in a different setup. This way I could compare each batch and see what similarities existed, which I could then usually attribute to the actual strain itself. After sampling several batches of a given strain, I would then have a good idea of what the strain should be like, and my review of the strain could then begin.

As far as judging flavor, aroma, and type of high, this is all completely subjective, and everybody has different preferences. In order to make things as fair as possible, I would sit in a circle of fellow connoisseurs and pass joints and bubblers around, asking everybody to describe the flavors and highs that they were experiencing. Certain points we would all agree on. These are what got printed in *The Cannabible* most often. The staggeringly wide array of possibilities that exist within the cannabis gene pool, and various breeders' appreciation of these different possibilities, partly explain why there are so many cannabis strains in existence.

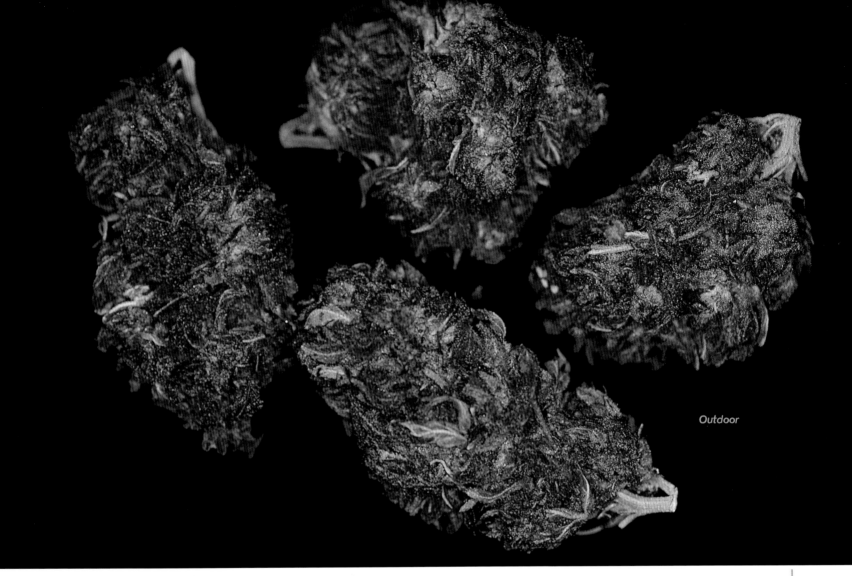

Outdoor

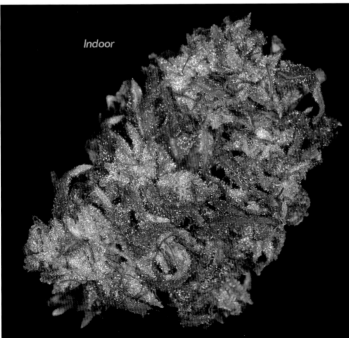

Indoor

Cough

Cough is a spicy Haze hybrid from the West Coast—
a tropical and delicious nugget indeed. Lush and spicy,
she is reminiscent of Kali Mist, yet fatter and with a little
more body. The high is up and giggly, and long-lived as
well. I was baked for four hours after smoking some.
Shown are indoor and outdoor samples, both grown
organically in soil. The outdoor sample is from Grass
Valley, California. And yes, I coughed plenty.

| 51

Dawg

The story goes some advanced organic growers got a hold of the fabled Chem strain (see page 46) and were determined to prove that it could be just as good or better when grown organically. The **Dawg** is the result of this experiment. They melded with the plant, paying close attention to the minute details, and developed an organic system of growning the Chem that produced incredible herb. Once they had it down organically, it seemed that they could no longer call it the Chem. So the organic version of the Chem then became known as the Dawg. As much as I would like to say that it's better than the chemmy Chem, it's just not. The flavor is wonderful, an earthy, robust, peatlike flavor—but it's not as flavorful as the Chem. The high is extremely strong. It gave me loss of coordination and made my eyes red, but again, it's not as strong as the Chem. Go figure.

Diesel (#2, #7, #10)

In the first volume of *The Cannabible,* we saw the original New York City Diesel. Here we have three other **Diesel** phenotypes, #2, #7, and #10. Although the #7 and the #10 are both excellent, the #2 is the winner by far. Diesel #2 tastes almost identical to the New York City Diesel featured in volume 1. It's this greasy, petrol-candied tinge that is disturbingly good. Unfortunately, she takes the longest to grow and harvests the least of the three. But, in her defense, the taste and high are magnificent. The high is warped and giggly, causing my eyelids to drop by 50 percent. All three phenotypes were grown indoors organically in soil in North Carolina, and all three were much better than Soma's weak "unleaded" Diesel hybrid. There has been much debate about Diesel's origins. The story I'm most inclined to believe is that it comes from an old Mexican strain from Oaxaca. Approximately twenty years ago in New York City, a clone was taken from this legendary Mexican, and this clone is what we now call Diesel.

Diesel #2

Diesel #2

Diesel #2

53

Diesel #7

Diesel #7

Diesel #10

54

Diesel #10

Diesel X Malawi X Diesel

This bud, grown outdoors organically in Humboldt, California, got me so ridiculously high that I could barely take a correctly focused photo. Malawi, Africa, is known to have cannabis strains containing high levels of THCV, a rare and particularly psychedelic component of certain strains. I believe this warped Malawi cross definitely contained high THCV levels. I temporarily became very stupid from this herb, which is not normal for me. I got lost several times, bumped into things, and had a shit-eating grin on my face the entire time. Scary. Grown outdoors organically in Northern California.

Effects of Legalization

Many a debate has been had over whether legalization of marijuana would affect the profits of those who make so much on it now. Many growers/smugglers/dealers actually want the herb to stay illegal, as it has provided them with a very prosperous lifestyle as is. Ironically, these are the people with enough money (power) to actually get the herb legalized, if they wished. All it takes is money. As an example, many people do not realize that Proposition 215, which legalized medicinal marijuana in California, was passed mainly because of a couple of large donations by George Soros and Dennis Peron to pay for petitioners and so forth. The main reason marijuana is still illegal is that the industries that stand to lose billions if it were legalized (alcohol, tobacco, pharmaceuticals, etc.) donate huge amounts of money to politicians that support their agendas—that is, keeping marijuana illegal. The brutal irony here is that these same companies stand to *make* billions when it becomes legal.

Please don't make the mistake of believing that the tobacco companies aren't poised to pounce on the mass-produced commercial schwag situation. As early as 1993, Philip Morris filed trademark applications for "Marley" brand cannabis cigarettes. (I can't think of a worse insult to the Marley name, personally.) Other tobacco companies registered names such as "Acapulco Gold" and "Red Leb," and in 1998, it was revealed that British American Tobacco had secret plans to introduce cigarettes laced with "subliminal" amounts of ganja if it were ever legalized.

You can pretty much be assured that "Big Pharma" has been working on THC-based preparations and are ready to flood the patent and trademark office with patent applications once it is legalized. This will mean that any method or process for the preparation of a THC-based compound, as well as the compound itself, could become the property of Merck, for example, for twenty years. It is disturbing to think about the possibility of a new genetically modified strain patented by Monsanto. Theoretically, all strains would be "new" once legalized. Translation: Monsanto, for example, could own the rights to any of your favorite strains.

Despite this, legalized marijuana would not take the profits from those who have been doing so well with it up to now. To prove my point, we can look at history. In the 1970s, when good-quality herb was abundant and cheap, with ounces going for $10 to $20, super-high-grade herb, such as Original Haze, went for as much as $200 an ounce. You simply cannot mass-produce top-quality ganja. Producing herb of this legendary quality requires too much care and attention in the drying, manicuring, and curing processes for this. This level of attention, as well as the careful handling required, is simply not possible when the harvest is in the tons. These are very delicate flowers, I remind you. As another example, let's take a look at microbrewed beer. Even though anyone can go out and get a case of cheap beer for 50¢ a can, countless people purchase $12 and up six-packs of small-batch specialty microbrews every day. And beer is legal! Now think of how much money people spend on $100 and up bottles of (legal) wine every single day! And cigars!

Yes, surely the price would come down if ganja were legal, even for the best stuff, but legality would allow much more to be produced, which would more than offset the difference. Add to that the ability to grow it without the fear of being locked in a cage, and you will see my point. I envision a world with legal ganja, and just as one would be able to purchase cheap, mass-produced, pre-rolled joints, one could also purchase expensive specialty herb, exotic and unique strains grown lovingly in small batches. There will always be a market for top-quality, organic ganja. The history of economics and the laws of supply and demand dictate this. The days of legal ganja are coming, so let's all give thanks for that.

This is a call to all the people who have made a fortune from the herb: it's time to give back! If every dealer in America gave one week's worth of their profits to solid foundations such as NORML (www.norml.org), Drug Policy Alliance/Lindesmith Center (www.lindesmith.org), Marijuana Policy Project (www.mpp.org), Vote Hemp (www.votehemp.com), and so forth, it would be done. Marijuana would be legalized almost instantly. If every smoker in America went without a bag for a week and instead donated this money to one of the above-named organizations, this would also be more than enough. The time has come! Too many of our brothers and sisters, our mothers and our fathers sit in cages simply for their desire to enjoy God's sweetest flower! This must be stopped!

A lovely indoor, organic Big Bud garden ready to be harvested.
This is the real Big Bud, the one for all other Big Buds to aspire to.

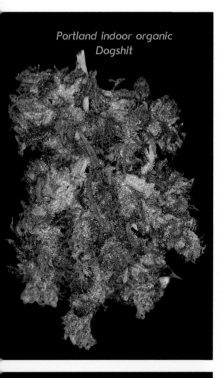

Portland indoor organic Dogshit

California outdoor Dogshit

58

Dogshit

Not to be confused with Catpiss from the first volume of *The Cannabible*, **Dogshit** is also an actual strain. Luckily, the plants only smell like dogshit right as they go into flowering. The finished product smells more like high-grade cannabis. These plants, grown in the full California sun, were absolute monsters. Some exceeded four pounds of dried flowers. The "Redneck Ridge" clan, as they like to be called, had large holes dug with a backhoe, which they filled with a mixture of cow and chicken manure, and then planted the DS. Six months later—well let's just say that there is enough medicine for a while. Another highly successful medical grow of Northern California. Also shown is the legendary Pacific Northwest Dogshit, which seemed entirely unrelated to the California version. The Portland Dogshit has a thick, pungent medicinal flavor and produced a pounding buzz.

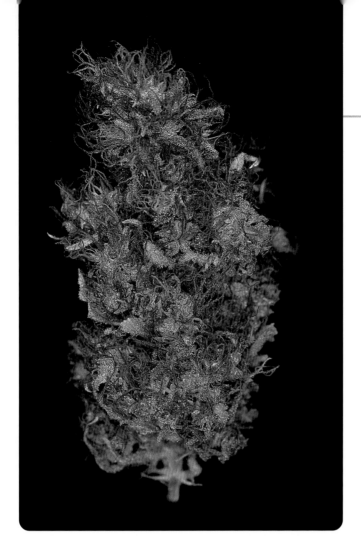

Dynamite

Dynamite is a super-potent indica that I came across while bud hunting in the Pacific Northwest. She has a delightful pungent and hashy flavor, albeit a little harsh and overpowering at times. The high is a bit cloudy for my personal tastes, but many people prefer narcotic-feeling indicas. This one was grown indoors organically in soil. I have never seen this strain anywhere else, and it's not in any seed catalogs to my knowledge.

Early Sativa

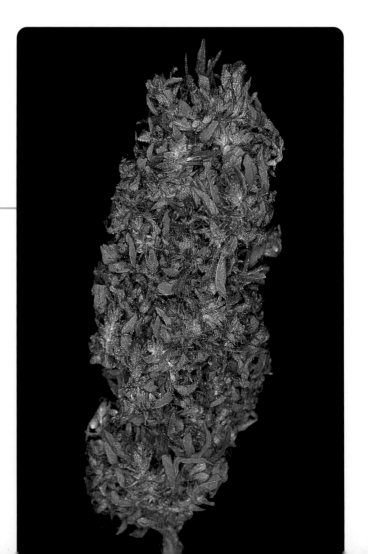

This wonderfully delicate sativa was grown outdoors, organically, in Oregon. Grassy and vitaminy in flavor, these buds were a blast from the past, reminding me of some of the first homegrown I ever smoked. The high is clear and mild, perfect for mornings or lightweights. Coming from the Great White Northern Seed Company, this compact and hardy sativa bush will harvest by September 1st, making it great for guerilla growing.

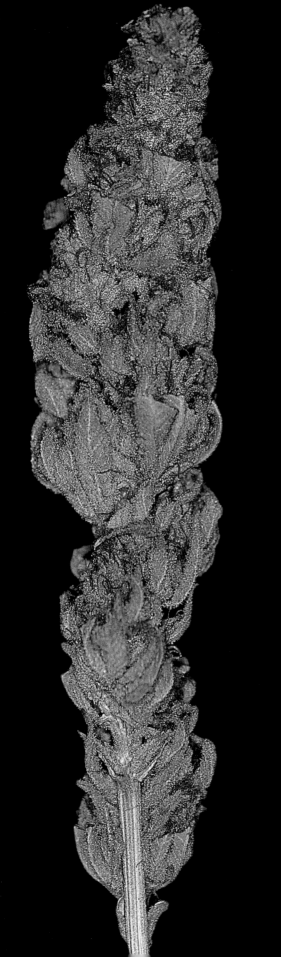

Emerald Triangle Funk X Purple Oregon Sativa

Someone really needs to come up with a name for this one! These gorgeous nugs, coming from Nebu's collection, smell like—well, hippy minus the B.O. It's a yummy scent of sage, incense, and kind bud. These buds were over two years old, vacuum-sealed at the peak of their curing process. Vegan and organically grown indoors in soil, this strain has a delicious Thai flavor with rich, earthy, purple tones. Although the resin glands are small, there are gazillions of them, and this strain is very stoney. The high is up, conversational, and highly thought pro-voking. Also shown below is the same strain with California Orange bred into the mix. This added a wonderful citrus quality to the herb, easily detectable to the discerning palate.

Marijuana Smoking and Creativity

Scores of people, especially musicians and artists, are attracted to the creativity-enhancing qualities of marijuana. What is it about this magical plant that inspires so many people's creativity? Many people experience a deeper ability to concentrate, more open-mindedness, heightened confidence, and lessened inhibitions after smoking marijuana—all wonderful boosts to the creative process. As a musician, I can tell you that my musical skills are greatly enhanced after enjoying some herb. My creativity soars, and I become much more nimble on the keys. Most importantly, ganja allows me to clear my mind and focus completely on the music at hand. It allows me to reach a meditative place that is next to impossible to achieve without medicating (or meditating) first. In all honesty, I rarely enjoy playing without THC involved. My mind is in fifty places at once, and the music suffers as a result. As soon as I take a puff, a major shift happens. I am able to focus every bit of my attention on my playing, and the results are dramatic. It comes as no surprise that many of history's finest musicians were high.

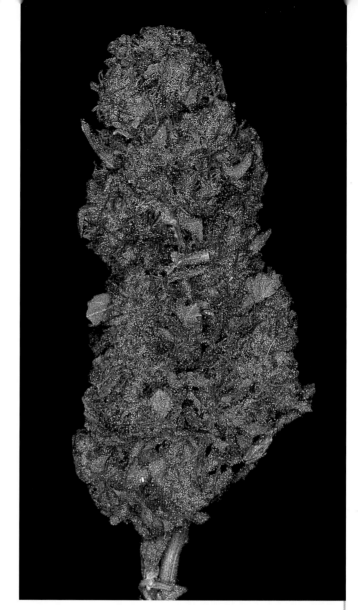

Five-0

Coming from the British Columbia Seed Company, **Five-0** is a hybridized cross of Hawaiian Indica and Northern Lights #5. This mostly indica herb is strong to say the least, and quite tasty as well. There is a satisfying hashy and slightly tropical flavor, and due to its competent grower and completely organic cultivation, it tastes great down to the end of a bowl or joint. This herb gave me stimulating cranial sensations that were quite pleasant. She was grown organically indoors in soil in Eureka, California.

Foggy Mountain

This gorgeous strain, grown outdoors organically from seed in the full California sunlight, was impressive in all attributes. These farmers are religious about being 100 percent organic, and this is evident when puffing on some of this super smooth and savory herb. The complex flavor, best appreciated in a big fatty or perhaps a vaporizer, is sour grape, with definite apple tones as well. There is also a smooth mentholated characteristic, evident mostly upon the exhale. The high is warm and giggly, a little foggy, and not at all lacking in strength.

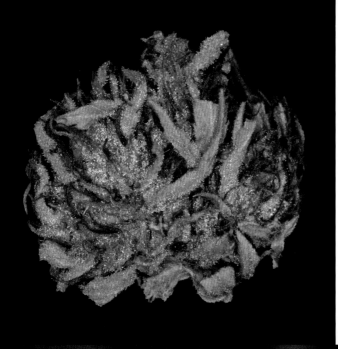

Fruit

Fruit is a twenty-five-year-old Maui sativa that has a mouth-wateringly lush and tropical flavor that very much resembles Hawaiian Punch fruit drink. This exotic sativa has a heavenly aroma that is absolutely sublime. Aromatic hints of chewed bubblegum, mango, grape, and several other tropical fruits assault the olfactory sense. The high is strong and fairly warped, even giggly at times.

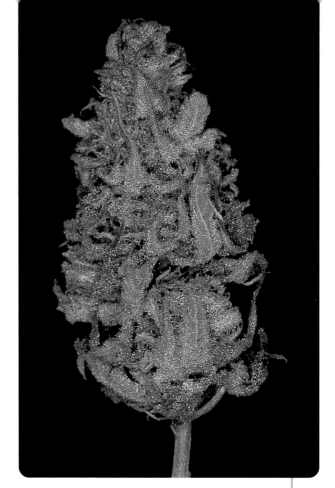

Genius

Genius is a female Jack Herer phenotype, developed by the Brothers Grimm Seed Company, and used to create Apollo 11, Cinderella 99, and several others. The Brothers call it the "Royal Line," and these genetics are indeed top rate all around. The energetic, thought-provoking high that Genius provides makes her highly desirable, and fantastic breeding material. Her tangy lemon Pledge scent is also quite desirable. This particular sample was grown indoors.

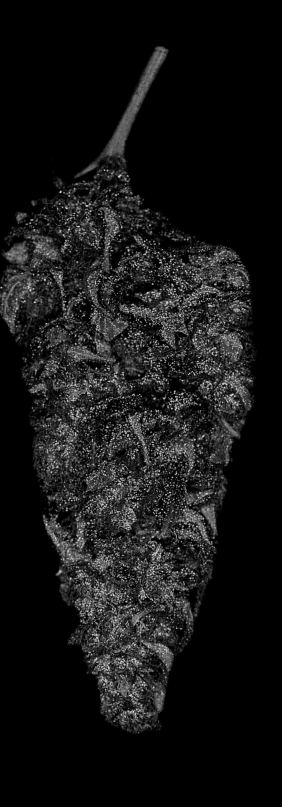

Grape

Coming by way of Tallahassee, Florida, **Grape** is a favorite among Eugene, Oregon, connoisseur circles. This hybrid, bred from standard Amsterdam genetics, exists only as a clone now, and produces luscious satiny grape flavors that are simply mouthwatering. The high is relatively strong, emanating from the chest area and expanding outward. These ladies were grown organically indoors in soil, evident by the rich and smooth tones of flavor that graced my taste buds.

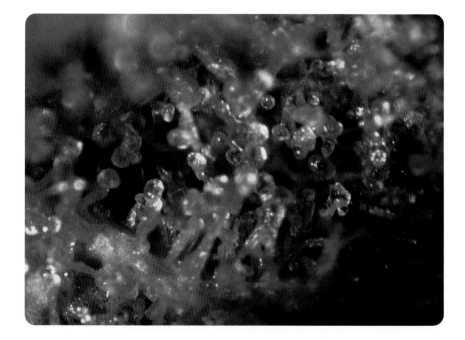

Grapefruit X Afghani

Here we have **Grapefruit**, a popular Canadian strain, crossed with a standard **Afghani** indica. Grown outdoors organically in California, these buds have a mild dry and citrusy flavor, with tones of hashish also noticeable. The high is cloudy and sedative, not at all my personal favorite.

Grapefruit X Chemo

Here is another lovely **Grapefruit** hybrid, this time crossed with the legendary **Chemo,** an extremely potent B.C. indica strain rumored to have been developed by the Canadian government as a medicine for cancer patients. This herb was wickedly good, with sublime tangy citrus notes and a powerful narcotic buzz.

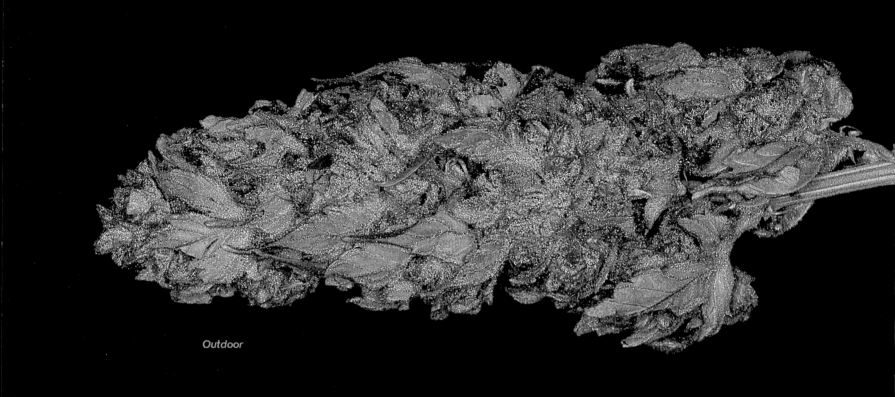

Outdoor

73

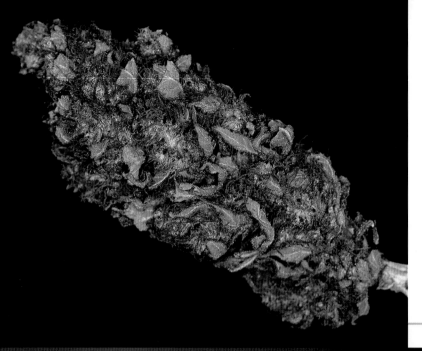

Grunk

Grunk is a hybridized cross of Grape (see page 68) and Skunk (see the first volume of *The Cannabible*). The Grape is an old Florida strain that has a very easily distinguished grape flavor and a strong sativa high. The Skunk used was the classic West Coast Skunk #1. This offspring is Grape dominant, with soft and sensual purplish tones of grapiness that delight the palate. The high is meditative and contemplative, very much mental candy.

Grown indoors organically in soil in Eugene, Oregon, home to some of the finest herb on the planet.

Hasan

Presumably named after Hasan ibn al-Sabbah, the leader of the Assassins, an unorthodox Muslim sect in the year 1090. This indoor, hydroponically grown indica would have been much more enjoyable had it not been pumped up with chemicals. I was unable to appreciate this gooey indica as a result of this.

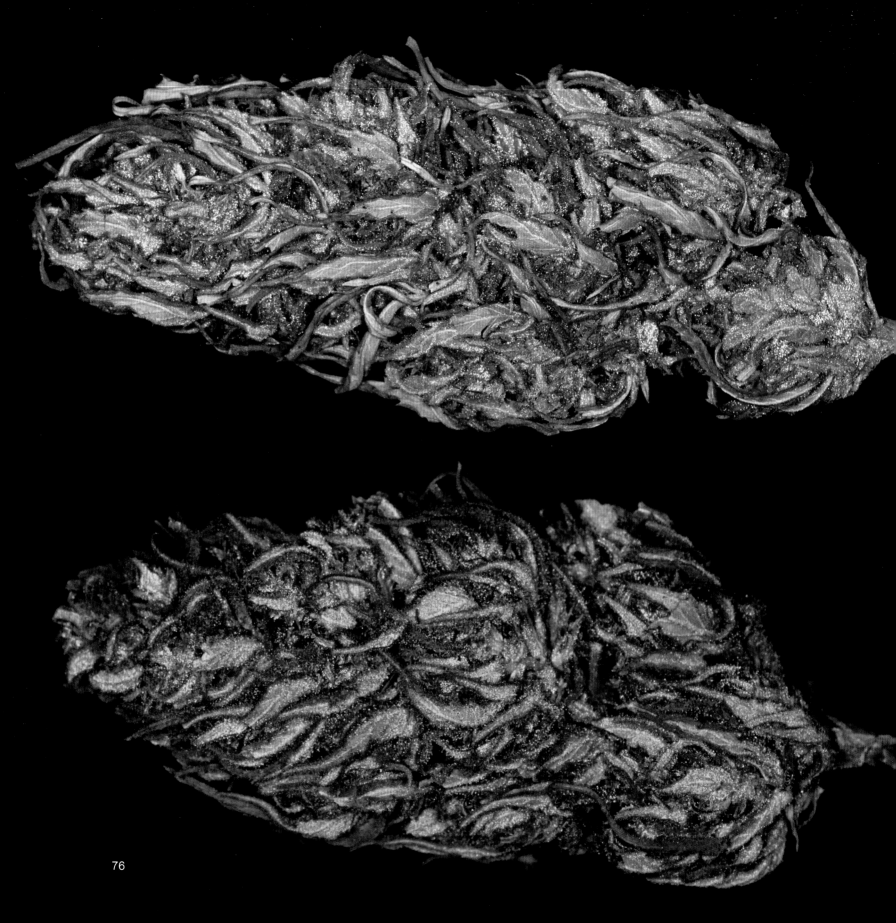

Haze

Pictured are two different **Haze** buds. These outdoor California-grown sativas are quite complex in character. Emitting a fragrantly eucalyptus and almost sour smell on the squeeze, these nugs were also mentholated and left my nose tingling. The flavor is quite different—earthy and spicy, like a good Haze should be. Very clear and up, the high was perfect for daytime.

Heroauna

If there was one strain in the first volume of *The Cannabible* that people wanted to see more of, it was **Herouana**. Well, here we have a gorgeous live Heroauna plant that was grown indoors organically in soil. Also shown is a live microscopic photo of the same plant

Holland's Hope

One of the first Dutch outdoor strains, **Holland's Hope** has been grown in Holland since the early '80s. A heavy indica variety with a narcotic stone, this particular batch was grown indoors organically in soil on the East Coast of the U.S. Known for being very mold resistant, Holland's Hope is a nice solid indica, if that's what you like. The flavor is herbal and slightly skunky, though a little bland.

Island Sweet Skunk

Federation Seeds takes the credit for this luscious and extremely yummy, mostly sativa strain. This one is extremely vigorous and easy to grow. She has a flavor that hits with tones of fruit punch, grapefruit, bubblegum, and skunk all at once. It's quite an experience. The high is also excellent, a warm and happy buzz that is all at once gentle and euphoric.

79

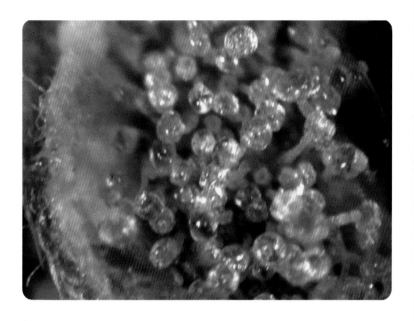

Jack Candy

Another of Nebu's fine vegan selections, these buds were so spicy and tropical tasting that they really reminded me of good Hawaiian *pakalolo*. An F2 selection from Sensi's '98 Jack Flash, **Jack Candy** produced a high that was clean, clear, and very happy.

Jamaica

the ganja in Jamaica ranges from brown schwag to greenish, skunky, dank bud. On the streets, one can easily pay $100 for a half ounce of crap, assuming you are not completely ripped off. But with a better connection, a pound of good-quality ganja can be procured for under $100. The cannabis genetics in Jamaica are excellent, with old Jamaican strains comingling with newer Amsterdam genetics. The failing in Jamaican herb is in the drying and curing. Most ganja is hung outside to dry, where it turns brown and loses at least half the flavor and potency. Add to this the fact that it is usually handled very roughly, and possibly rubbed for hash as well, and you will understand my point.

Many of Jamaica's older strains come from Colombia, logical due to proximity as well as the island's position along well-established smuggling routes to Florida.

Jamaica is extremely polluted, violently dangerous, and ridiculously expensive as well. Despite the availability of cheap and quality ganja, I cannot in good faith recommend a Jamaican vacation to my readers. There are much better destinations, in my opinion.

81

Jamaican hash

Brother LeeRoy Campbell, a major force behind the Jamaican legalization movement. Contact LeeRoy at friendsint@hotmail.com.

Lambsbread

Purple Jamaican Skunk

Jamaica

85

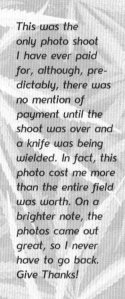

This was the only photo shoot I have ever paid for, although, predictably, there was no mention of payment until the shoot was over and a knife was being wielded. In fact, this photo cost me more than the entire field was worth. On a brighter note, the photos came out great, so I never have to go back. Give Thanks!

Jamaica

These were all short-season plants, each harvesting only about a half ounce.

Top Seven Cannabis Tourism Destinations

Cannabis tourism is becoming ever more popular. Prerequisites for a country to be on this list include the following:

1. Easy availability of cannabis
2. Affordable price
3. Acceptable quality
4. Relaxed laws

So here is a look at the top seven cannabis destinations on the planet.

Amsterdam

Topping the cannabis tourism destinations' list is beloved Amsterdam, with hundreds of "coffee shops" selling small amounts of marijuana and hashish over the counter for decades. These sales are not exactly legal, but they are very much tolerated, and as long as you are being respectful, you need not fear arrest or persecution in this highly civilized country. Prices for marijuana and hash in Holland range from US$3 to US$12 per gram, and sometimes higher for exotics. Quality ranges from mediocre to outrageous, and although the less than ideal weather conditions make the outdoor organic sativas that I prefer generally unavailable, one can very easily find something worth smoking.

Switzerland

See "The Swiss Experience," pages 160–61.

Spain

Although Spanish laws prohibit the use of cannabis, whether or not to arrest "offenders" is left to the discretion of the police, and they rarely do so. Personal possession is now legally defined as up to fifty grams. Ganja and hash are easily available in most cities, although mostly what is seen is low- to mid-grade Moroccan hashish. Marijuana is, however, becoming more popular. Spain's ideal growing conditions allow for the cultivation of excellent quality herb.

California

California has, since the '60s, been a top producer of world-class marijuana. Many of the world's top strains were created here, and an incredible variety of smoke is usually available. The medical marijuana scene has noticeably improved the quality and availability of connoisseur-grade stash. This factor, as well as competition from cheap but low-quality British Columbian herb, has brought down the prices, which now hover at about $300 for an ounce. Possession of an ounce or less is considered a misdemeanor and is usually punished with a small fine or warning.

Australia (Nimbin!)

Australia grows some seriously kick-ass herb. It is widely available in most places, especially Nimbin, a funky alternative community in New South Wales. In comparison to the prices in the U.S., Aussie herb is very reasonable. Sweet tropical "bush" sativas can be had for US$75 to US$125 an ounce. Indoor grown is available as well; however it is considerably more expensive and not as good, in my opinion. Cannabis laws vary from state to state; however, if one is caught with fifteen grams or less, the police have the power to issue cautions rather than going to court. Most often, a small fine or simple confiscation of the herb is the result.

British Columbia

B.C. is a major cannabis haven, and although most of the B.C. bud we see in America is schwaggy mass-produced hydro, some fantastic herb, both indoors and out, can easily be procured in B.C. Canada is minutes away from complete legalization it seems, and one can feel safe when puffing in this gorgeous place. Prices are very reasonable as well, and rapidly dropping as legalization gets closer.

Christiania (Denmark)

Christiania, also known as "Free Town," is a charming squat in the city of Copenhagen, a sociological experiment that has its own set of laws—and soft drugs are legal. On "Pusher's Street," one can easily purchase a wide variety of herb and hash (as well as other soft drugs) for prices about half of what we pay in the U.S. There is a lovely lake to paddle on in the summer, as well as an abundance of freaky cool dogs to trip out on. The hypocritical police occasionally make raids, but usually only the dealers get harassed.

Sunset in Australia

KC 33

KC Brains Holland Seed Company takes the credit for this sweet ganja strain. It's said to be an old Dutch strain crossed with Thai and Brazilian male plants. This nug had a high-toned citrusy aroma leaning toward lemon. The high is about average, perhaps a bit stronger. This batch was grown organically indoors in soil.

KGB

Here we have a fine strain from Vancouver Island Seed Company, **KGB**. This Afghani X Burmese hybrid has a unique flavor, resembling the smell of a wine barrel. It's tangy and oaky and very enticing, with lots of indescribable undertones. The high is full and bright and quite up for a mostly indica. I look forward to seeing more from this seed company.

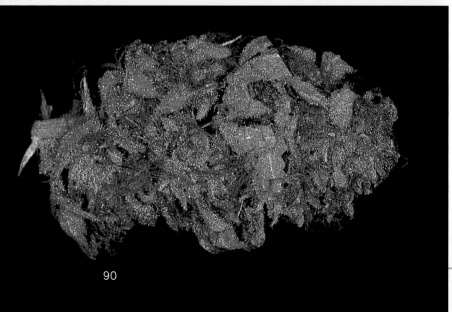

Here we have a solid indica/sativa hybrid local to Southern California. She was grown outdoors organically and has a mild herbal flavor with a slight suggestion of flowers and mint. The high is also mild, but quite pleasant, ideal for lightweights or a daytime smoke.

L.A. Rose

91

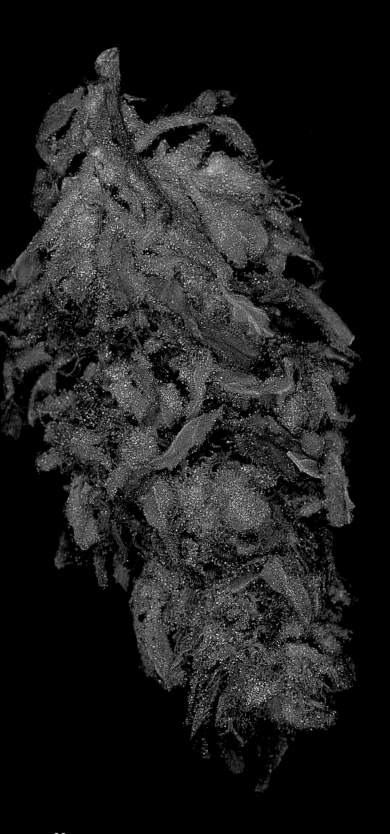

LemonAde 2000

This lovely California outdoor-grown strain has a lineage that breaks down as follows: **Lemon-Ade** X Brothers Grimm C88 X Killer Queen. There is a definite pink-lemony smell, and luckily it tastes as good as it smells. I could swear I tasted pink lemonade. Thick, tangy, and extremely expanding smoke left me with a piercing buzz that lasted half the day. This strain is a favorite among many of the people who grow or smoke it.

Livity

These monster-sized plants were grown in full, intense sunlight in Northern California. Coming from the Apothecary Seed Company, **Livity's** lineage is as follows: Pez X Cherry Bomb. As you might have guessed, there is a pronounced cherry flavor inherent in these plants. There is also a wonderful menthol quality to the strain. The high of Livity is mild yet effective, making it a very pleasing daytime herb.

Livity

Marijuana versus Wine

Many similarities exist between the appreciation of wine and the appreciation of cannabis. In fact, many of the techniques used to distinguish and appreciate wine can be applied to cannabis. There is, however, one major difference. Wine has many different flavors and bouquets to appreciate, but, quite frankly, on judging the effects, it's all the same drunkenness. You will never hear a wine connoisseur boasting about the killer buzz that his favorite Chardonnay packs. It's all the same. With marijuana, however, not only do we get to appreciate every conceivable flavor and aroma, but Mother Nature was also thoughtful enough to vary the effects of each strain, providing an infinite array of different highs to satisfy all our medicinal and recreational needs. This is where marijuana leaves wine in the dust. It opens up a whole new level of appreciation that just does not exist within wine (or any alcohol for that matter). This partly explains why many wine connoisseurs only smell and sip the wine and then spit it out. Perhaps this is what a certain ex-president was trying to achieve when he allegedly didn't inhale.

Mexican Sativa

Love Potion #9

Coming from a seed company known as the Joker Collection, this mostly indica is reportedly a Love Potion #5 crossed with a Northern Lights male. Hybrid vigor is present, with a larger yield and stronger potency than either parent. Grown outdoors organically in southern Humboldt, this girl has an exotic perfumed floral character, and a stony, head-tingly euphoric buzz.

Matanuska Mist

A favorite among many a West Coast connoisseur, **Matanuska Mist** is a cross of the legendary Alaskan Matanuska Thunderfuck (see the first volume of *The Cannabible*) and Grey Area Coffeshop's Grey Mist. This one is fast gaining popularity with indoor growers around Humboldt, California, which is where this batch was grown. The flavor is soft, spicy, and sweet—very enjoyable to say the least. The smoke is quite expansive, so hold on tight. The high is a major creeper, and eventually it will catch up with you. Perfect for enjoying after a long day's whatever.

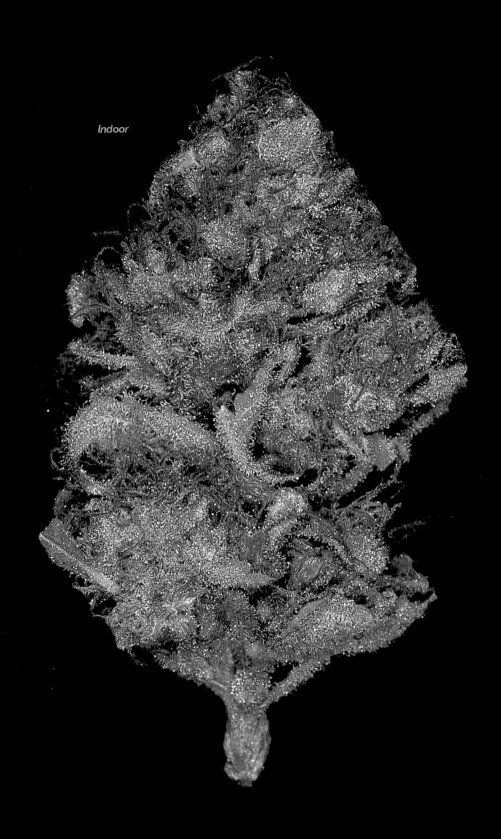

Indoor

Maui Wowie II

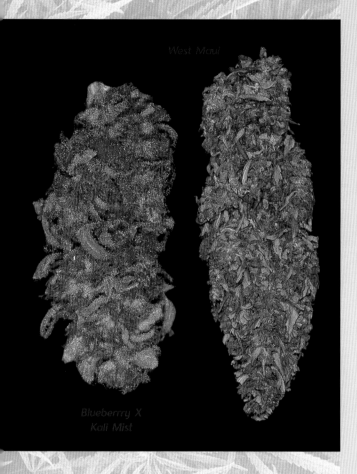

West Maui

Blueberrry X
Kali Mist

no *Cannabible* volume would be complete without a luscious spread of Maui Wowie. As far as I can tell, there never was one particular strain that was the end-all Maui Wowie. This name generally refers to any good Maui bud. Hawaiian herb is my favorite on the planet, due to its mouthwatering tropical flavors and warped psychedelic highs. Due to extreme helicopter raids and other various obstacles, top-quality Maui bud is not easily available. To score some almost requires that you live in the islands, and even that is no guarantee! It is, however, worth the wait! There is a saying on Maui: *"No Ka Oi."* It means, "It's the best." I can almost guarantee they're talking about the local *pakalolo!* (Hawaiian for "Crazy Weed").

Hawaiian Skunk

98

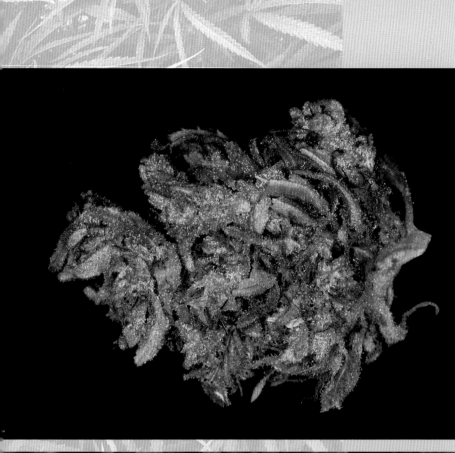

DJ Shorts Flo grown outdoors organically in Maui, Hawaii

Maui
Wowie II

Maui Outdoor

101

Mendocino Greenhouse

this greenhouse was home to some of the most humongous plants I've ever seen. Multiple unnamed strains were present, mostly grown from seeds pulled out of the best stash from the year before. This garden was completely organic, and the variety of strains was quite impressive. The full gamut of indicas and sativas could be spotted, and some of those sativas topped fifteen feet. These kind growers were busted the year before and grew this garden on the very same land, as they awaited trial. I am happy to inform you that not only did they pull off this magnificent crop, but the judge threw out the case and it never went to trial!

103

Mendocino

Greenhouse

Mighty Mite X Durban

Mighty Mite is a fifteen-year-old British Columbian indica strain with origins in the Himalayas. She has a lovely pine smell, and when crossed with a **Durban** sativa from Africa, becomes even mightier. Grown outdoors in California, this hybrid made a nice daytime smoke, although it left me craving something more.

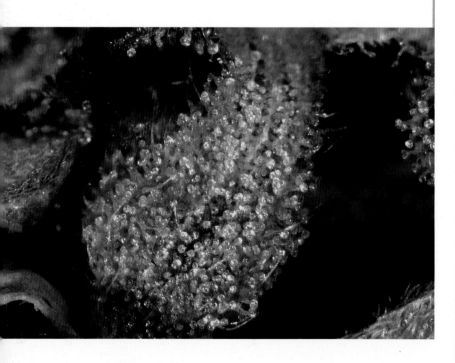

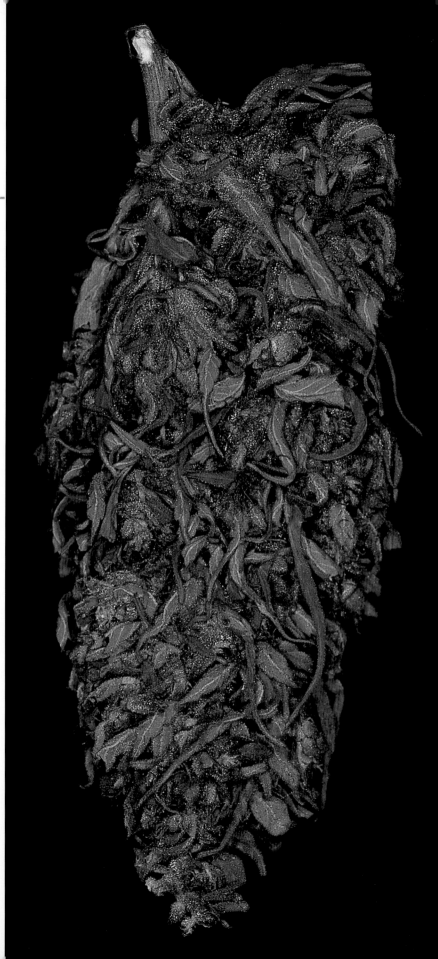

The Tolerance Factor

One strange and frustrating phenomenon that unfortunately affects marijuana smokers is the tolerance factor. If you smoke enough of a certain strain, or combination of strains, you will soon get "immune" to that strain/combo. I don't care if you're smoking 60 percent THC bubble hash dipped in honey oil and then rolled in kief, if you've been smoking primarily that combination for a while, you will get mostly immune to it (trust me, I've been there). After a few days, most likely it will barely get you high. But if you then smoke some other random bud that may not even be particularly good, you will probably get much higher. This must be due to the different cannabinoid profiles of the different strains, and our bodies' (quickly) built-up tolerance to these profiles. The way I see it, there are only two ways to get around this enemy.

1. Have an unlimited supply of different strains available, perhaps twenty varieties at least, and switch every few days (living in Amsterdam is helpful for this).

2. Smoke less herb.

Crazy as it sounds, this actually works. For a new and occasional smoker, the surest way to getting higher is to smoke more herb. Then, after a while, this painful and ironic switch happens. Soon, you smoke so much herb that it barely gets you high at all anymore. Ironically, if you cut back and smoke *less* herb, it will actually get you higher. We live in a very mysterious world.

Supreme quality water-hash looks like brown sugar. Even at over 50% THC, smoke it for a while and the enemy— tolerance—sets in.

Molokai

This trip really made me realize that I have the best job in the world. Molokai, a small island in the Hawaiian chain, does not produce a lot of *pakalolo* (anymore). But the *pakalolo* that is grown there is of phenomenal quality. Interestingly, it was quite different from Maui or Big Island buds, although these islands are not far away. These exotic ladies were grown on platforms in the tops of trees, and reaching them with my gear was no easy (bare) feat. These were short-season plants, each producing a half ounce at best. Grown on Molokai for decades, these strains had extreme tropical flavors, and highs that were electric and psychedelic. They were consciously grown and 100 percent organic. *Major* yum.

Morning Star

This old Northern California pure indica strain became so gooey in a joint that halfway through, it sealed itself shut and refused to be smoked. Luckily, there was a bubbler nearby, although it took a few hours for that nasty-looking resin-soaked roach to get smoked, as this stuff is extraordinarily strong. The flavor is very difficult to describe on this one—there are no words in the English language that exist as of yet. Here are the closest ones: woody, earthy, almost musky, *strong!* This stuff made me sweat. Tested at just shy of 24 percent THC, this herb completed its flowering cycle in an impressive fifty days.

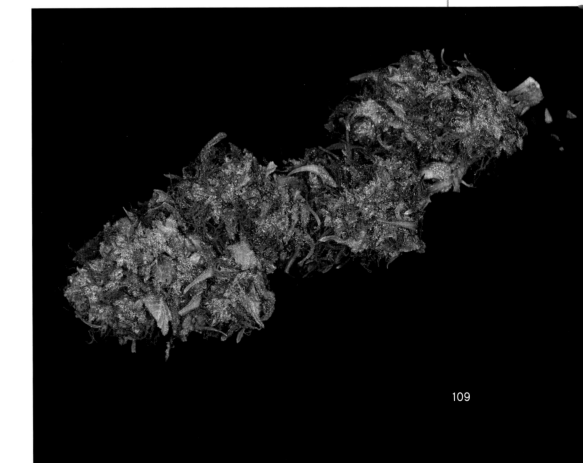

109

Mothership

The mothership has landed! Just when I thought that HP13 (see the first volume of *The Cannabible*) was the most flavorful strain on the planet, I was turned on to **Mothership**. Honestly, I can say it's a tie. They taste extremely similar. It's that same pungent, salty, skunky, hashy dankness that instantly makes you realize that most of the other pot out there is bland schwag. It's pretty much erotic. Although the flavor is very similar to HP13, it's perhaps a little less garlicky, a little more fruity, but just as flavorful and pungent. Growth characteristics, however, are extremely different. While HP13 is indica dominant, with a typical indica growth pattern, Mothership is a sativa, and a strange one at that. She likes to grow sideways through a garden, weaving her spectacular self through the other plants like a vine on a mission. Surprisingly, she is no slouch at all in either weight or harvest time. She is much quicker and heavier than one would expect from such an exotic sativa. I tried long and hard to get some info on her lineage, and all I could find out was that she came through Wyoming (of all places) and then on to the Carolinas and on to California. If I had to guess, I would say that Mothership is an HP13-Diesel cross, perhaps, but I could easily be wrong. If anyone out there knows, please tell me. Also shown is a sample grown organically outdoors in Northern California, which was outstanding beyond description. It was a pleasure to sample such an earthy Mothership. The strain retained its trippy "triple-tower" bud structure when grown outdoors, as well as its outrageously strong flavor.

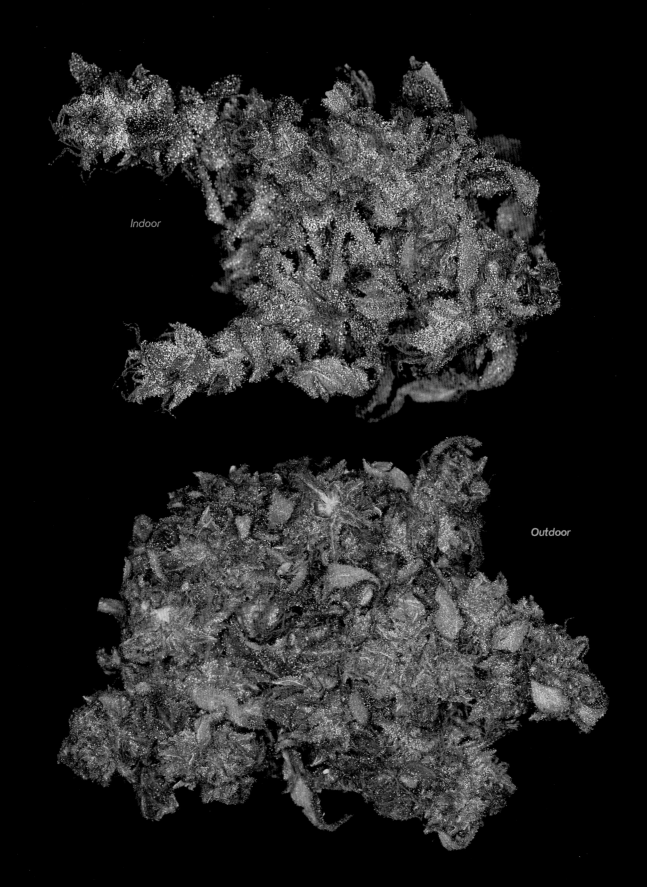

Indoor

Outdoor

111

Indoor organic

Indoor organic

Classy Glass 2

Netty

Netty is a California strain coming from the Lake Tahoe area, grown at over 6,000 feet in an organic hydro system. She is a cross of the original Champagne, a British Columbia indica, with Northern Lights. The flavor of this herb is like a mild Northern Lights, not overwhelming but decent. The high, however, is quite impressive. Strong and full spectrum, two hits of Netty were as effective as six of another strain.

Sonic Bloom

What if I told you there was a product that could potentially double the size of your harvest for under $80, and that the product was completely organic? This product is called Sonic Bloom. So far, I have only seen one ganja farmer using it, and this has got to change.

Sonic Bloom got its start in Korea in the '60s, when a young American soldier named Dan Carlson was horrified to witness a starving Korean woman place her child's legs under the back tire of an army truck, crippling the child and thereby entitling the family to a food subsidy from the government. In that horrific moment, Carlson dedicated his life to finding a way to help feed the starving masses of the world.

When he arrived back home, Carlson spent countless hours in the University of Minnesota library studying plant physiology. Working with the idea that certain sound frequencies might help plants breathe better, as well as absorb nutrients, Carlson and an audio engineer experimented with various frequencies until, after a stroke of spiritual insight, they found a combination of frequencies and harmonics that were identical to the predawn bird concerts that apparently help plants open their stomata wider. These stomata, or mouthlike pores, present in the thousands on every leaf, allow oxygen and water to transpire. Stomata are also used by plants to exchange aerosols and mists with the surrounding atmosphere. With the stomata in this extrareceptive state, plants are, by a factor of over 700 percent, more able to uptake nutrients.

After figuring out this ingenious method of getting plants to "open wide," Carlson began developing an organic nutrient spray to apply to the leaves while in this extremely receptive state. After fifteen years of trial and error, experimenting in labs throughout the country, Carlson produced the perfect formula. It includes sixty-four trace elements derived from natural products and seaweed, as well as chelated amino acids and growth stimulants. In addition, the surface tension of the water is altered to make it more easily absorbed.

The end result of all this fascinating research is sold as a kit called Sonic Bloom, and it includes a CD or cassette with these magical "birdsong frequencies" embedded within beautiful classical music, so as not to offend our sensitive ears. Also included is the nutrient spray, which is applied after forty-five minutes of playing the sounds for the plants. As you can see by the statistics below, one can expect vast improvements from using this ingenious product.

According to the producers of Sonic Bloom, plants become much more productive: Strawberry yields increase by 300 percent; apple yields increase by 50 percent; blueberries grow to be the diameter of a nickel and ripen two weeks sooner; soybean harvests double; cucumber plants produce three times as many cucumbers; hot peppers mature thirty days sooner and produce twice as many peppers; grape yields increase by 100 percent and sugars 2 percentage points; cranberries increase in size by 66 percent; tomato crops mature thirty-five days sooner and nearly double yields. Black walnut tree growth is accelerated 300 percent, making them ready for sale in twenty years instead of fifty years, chrysanthemum flowers double in quantity and mature in four weeks, and, potentially the most impressive growth statistic, Sonic Bloom produced a Purple Passion plant over 600 feet— a *Guinness Book* world record!

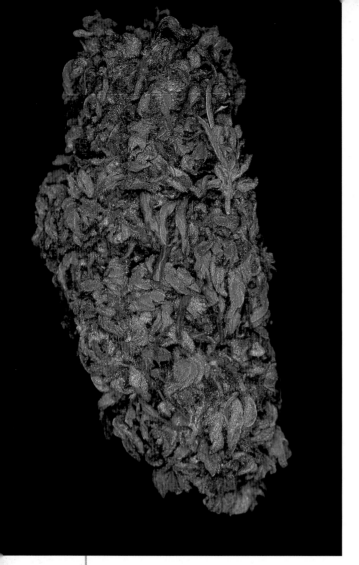

Northern Lights X Blueberry

Here we have two stunning versions of the ever-popular **Northern Lights X Blueberry:** an outdoor organic version from Northern California and an indoor organic soil version from North Carolina. Both were phenomenal, with the indoor version perhaps being a little more flavorful and the outdoor being a little more stony. (Indoor plants, which are considerably more protected from the elements than outdoor plants, can often be more flavorful than their outdoor counterparts. This is not, however, always the case—certain strains only taste really good when grown outdoors.) Delicious blueberry flavors were experienced in both samples, and the indica-dominant high from both was extremely heady and strong.

Ninja

This chunky indica was grown outdoors in Mendocino, California. When squeezed, it produces an indica pungency that reminds me of chewable vitamins. When burned, it produces rich, thick, powerful smoke with lovely woody (not Harrelson) flavors. The high is strong and felt heavily in the body as well as the head.

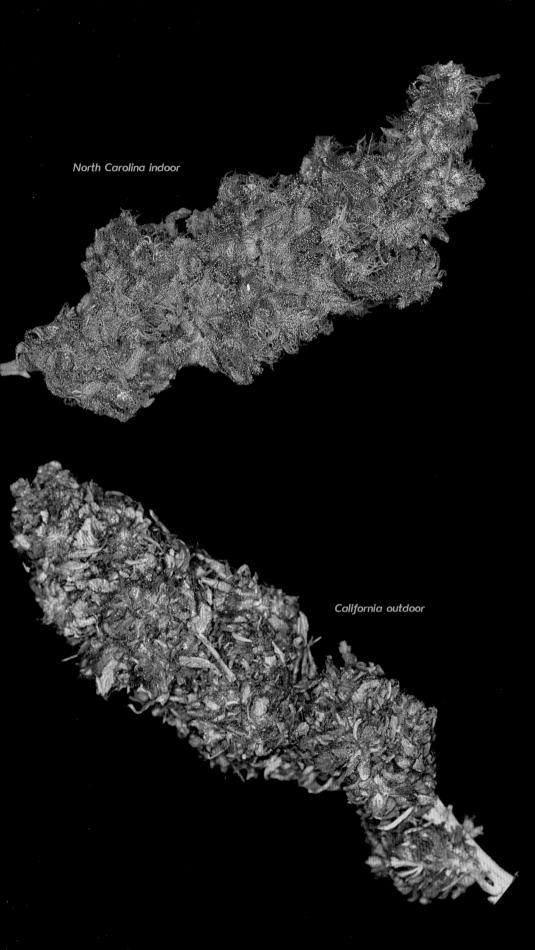

North Carolina indoor

California outdoor

California outdoor

119

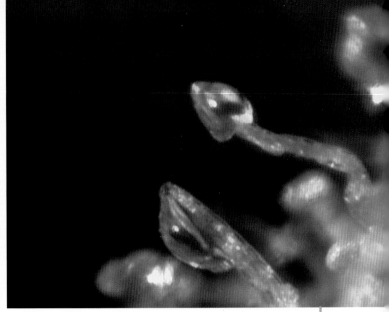

Omega

Omega, another Northern California–grown indica nugget, has a vitamin aroma when squeezed and, when smelled, slightly tickles the nose. With sweet and tangy smoke and a balmy red undertone, it made for a delicious smoke. The potency was average in all respects.

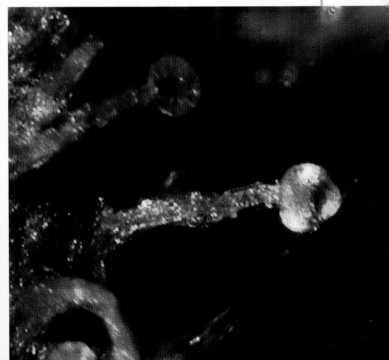

120

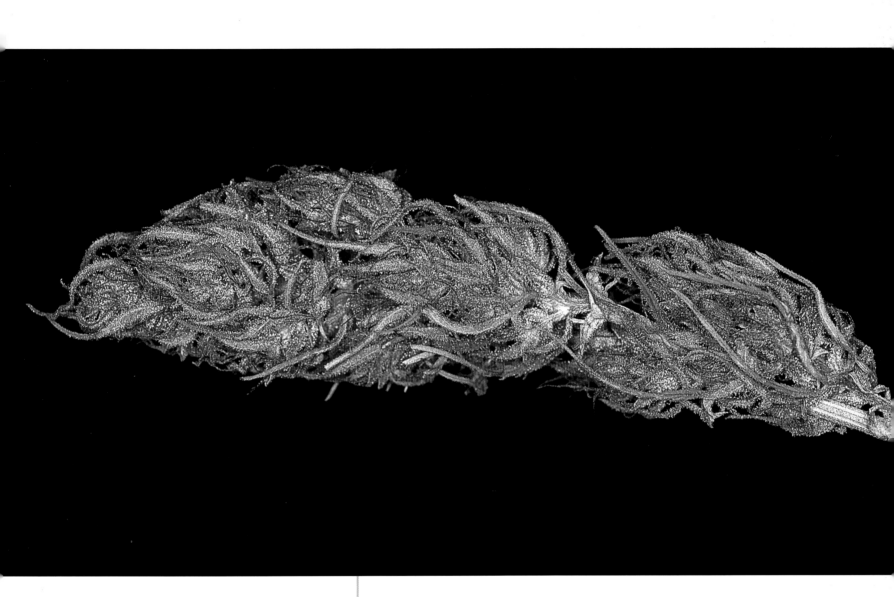

Oregon Sativa

Another sexy sativa from Oregon, this organically grown outdoor herb was light and delicious, with pleasant herbal flavors that were distant yet familiar. This ganja is very similar to many of the first sinsemilla crops grown in America in the '60s and early '70s. The genetics are most likely from Mexico, but this strain has been in Oregon for many years. The high is extremely clear and produced a subtle tingling sensation felt dancing up the spine.

Pakistani

This frosty indica was grown from seeds picked up just west of Quetta, on the Pakistan/Afghanistan border. These seeds were scored in 1991 and brought to southern Humboldt, where they have been grown since. Dusty and acrid in flavor, these indica buds were stony from head to toe, potency being at least average.

Pez

After attending the 2002 Seattle Hemp Fest, I photographed this grower's **Pez** crop. There were two different versions growing, one organic and one hydro. I predictably preferred the organic batch. This indica strain has a lovely candied nose to it, and luckily this flavor comes through in the smoke. Some of the plants truly smelled like Pez candy. Grown outdoors, Pez is a hearty strain, capable of surviving cold or rough conditions. Pez is now available from the Apothecary Seed Company.

State versus Federal Law

We live in very strange times. In the early days of our country, under the Articles of Confederation, the federal government was in charge of treaties with other countries, the navy, coordinating state militias in times of war, and other such national tasks. Everything else was governed by the states. After ten years, the Articles of Confederation were replaced by the U.S. Constitution. What most people didn't know then and don't know now is that Article 6 of the Constitution contains some legalese known as "the Supremacy Clause," which reads as follows:

> "This Constitution, and the Laws of the United States which shall be made in Pursuance thereof; and all Treaties made, or which shall be made, under the Authority of the United States, shall be the supreme Law of the Land; and the Judges in every State shall be bound thereby, any Thing in the Constitution or Laws of any state to the Contrary notwithstanding."

Translation: feds rule. Meaning, if your tomatoes are too big or small for federal law, for example, you can't sell them in the store (believe it or not, there is a federal law governing how big or small a tomato can be to be sold in a store). The same rule applies to ganja. A federal law says that marijuana is illegal, no matter what. Even state laws—such as California's Proposition 215, which "legalized" medical marijuana—are nullified by the Supremacy Clause. The state laws don't count, and you can't even mention them in federal court. So, basically, every time somebody gets prosecuted for medical marijuana, they can't mention anything about medical marijuana to the jury. Ed Rosenthal was even deputized by the City of Oakland to grow medical marijuana and to take advantage of a special federal law exemption for city officials. All of this was ruled irrelevant because of the Supremacy Clause. This leaves a medical marijuana defendant with only a "good character" defense, which at best leads to the low end of mandatory minimum sentencing guidelines, which are applied by the judge after conviction. The practical result is that medical marijuana patients and caregivers are left at the mercy of federal prosecutors. To make matters worse, if you exercise your First Amendment rights and get "too vocal" about medical marijuana, you are more likely to be prosecuted and imprisoned.

Although candidate George W. Bush claimed that states would be free to make their own decisions about the legality of medical marijuana, his Justice Department has taken exactly the opposite approach since the election. They have aggressively pursued civil and criminal actions against individuals and various groups associated with the medical marijuana movement. A spokesperson for the DEA recently told the Associated Press that "there is no such thing as medical marijuana. We're Americans first, Californians second." Interesting, considering voters in thirteen states have passed measures approving marijuana for medical use.

The solution is clear. We must amend the Constitution according to its terms to delete the Supremacy Clause and obtain local and state self-governance. Article 5 of the Constitution makes this possible. It reads as follows:

> "The Congress, whenever two-thirds of both Houses shall deem it necessary, shall propose Amendments to

this Constitution, or, on the Application of the Legislatures of two-thirds of the several States, shall call a Convention for proposing Amendments, which, in either Case, shall be valid to all Intents and Purposes, as Part of this Constitution, when ratified by the Legislatures of three-fourths of the several States, or by Conventions in three fourths thereof, as the one or the other Mode of Ratification may be proposed by the Congress; Provided that no Amendment which may be made prior to the Year One thousand eight hundred and eight shall in any Manner affect the first and fourth Clauses in the Ninth Section of the first Article; and that no State, without its Consent, shall be deprived of its equal Suffrage in the Senate."

So, everyone write to your state legislators and governors and ask for a resolution calling for an amendment to Article 6. When there are thirty-four state resolutions, we can get a constitutional convention. At the constitutional convention, you can amend the constitution by a vote of 75 percent, which is thirty-eight states.

Of course, what are the chances of this happening? Phat.

In July of 2003, the Hinchey-Rohrabacher bill, which aimed to bar the Department of Justice from challenging medical-marijuana laws in the states that have sanctioned medical-marijuana use lost (there are 10 states, including California). Still, the vote in the House was 273 to 152. That's progress from a 311 to 94 split in 1998.

Pineapple

Is there a fruit that exists that does not have a cannabis counterpart? I don't think so. Grown outdoors organically in Northern California, these lush nuggets have a flavor of several different tropical fruits, especially pineapple. There are also tantalizing pine and cedar tones, and a definite astringent quality. This complex ganja was very impressive—it finished first at a recent harvest festival that I was fortunate enough to attend. That says a lot. This strain is available in seed and clone form in Northern California.

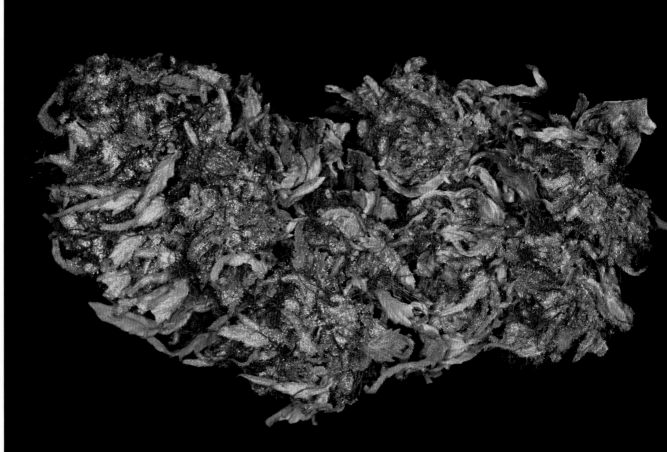

Pinetar

If you rub a stem of this gorgeous indica plant, your hand smells exactly like pine tar (hence the name). The flavor is piney, earthy, and slightly astringent. The high is very pleasant, not as overwhelming as some indicas can be. This plant was grown outdoors in Northern California.

Pod

This wickedly beautiful Maui-grown indica strain represents some of the most stunning ganja that I've ever seen. She's just as awesome as she looks, too. The **Pod** comes from an eastern Washington indica strain that has been tinkered with in Hawaii. The flavor is thick and hearty with strong hashy over-tones. The high is deva-statingly potent, almost head crushing, as one would imagine from the looks of this unique beautiful herb. Also shown is Daughter of Pod, below, which is a Washington Indica X Maui Sativa. Absolutely phe-nomenal, tropical, and ripping strong.

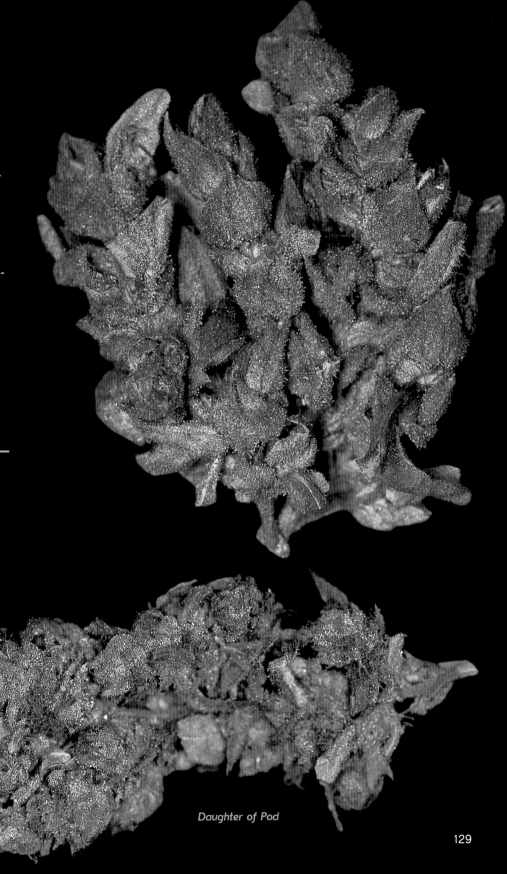

Daughter of Pod

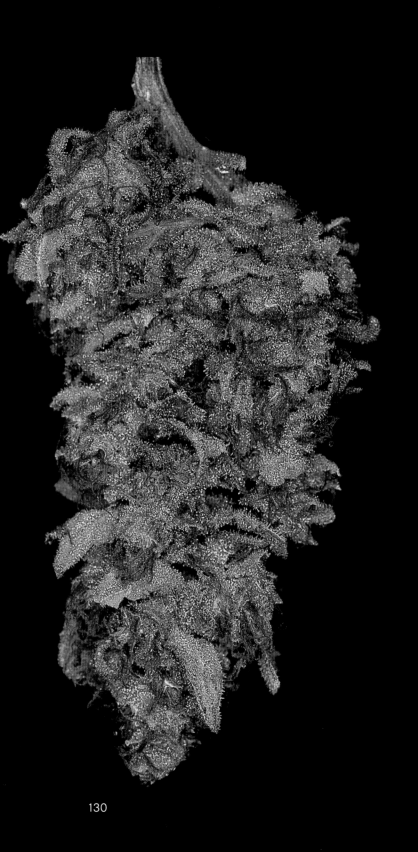

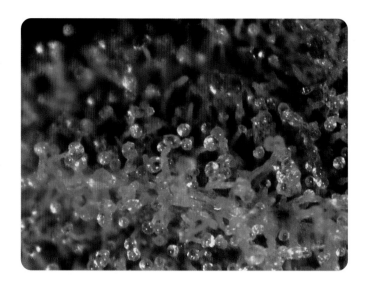

Princess Bob

This outdoor, organic, Maui-grown nug is a
good example of why I love the islands as I do.
You just don't get herb like this anywhere else.
Princess Bob comes from an eastern
Washington indica, similar to the Pod's ances-
try. The flavor is exactly like those little blue
marshmallows in BooBerry cereal, with hints of
papaya. The velvety flavor blooms and
mounts in a sublime crescendo, then lingers for
an eternity. The high is legendary as well. Powerful and psychedelic, it gave me light
hallucinations and an inability to stop laughing.

Purple FX

This stunning strain is a cross of The Purps (see page 135) and a strain simply called FX. I was extremely impressed with this strain, both the organic outdoor and the indoor hydro versions, which is rare for an organic freak like myself. The nose is similar to that of children's chewable vitamins (purple ones!). The flavor is so luscious and sublime, reminding me of high-quality flower essential oils such as lavender. The high is equally impressive. Highly euphoric and mentally stimulating, Purple FX quickly rose to the upper echelons of my favorite strains out there. Pictured are indoor hydro **Purple FX** as well as outdoor organic Purple FX. Also pictured is a hydroponically grown Purple FX X Big Bud.

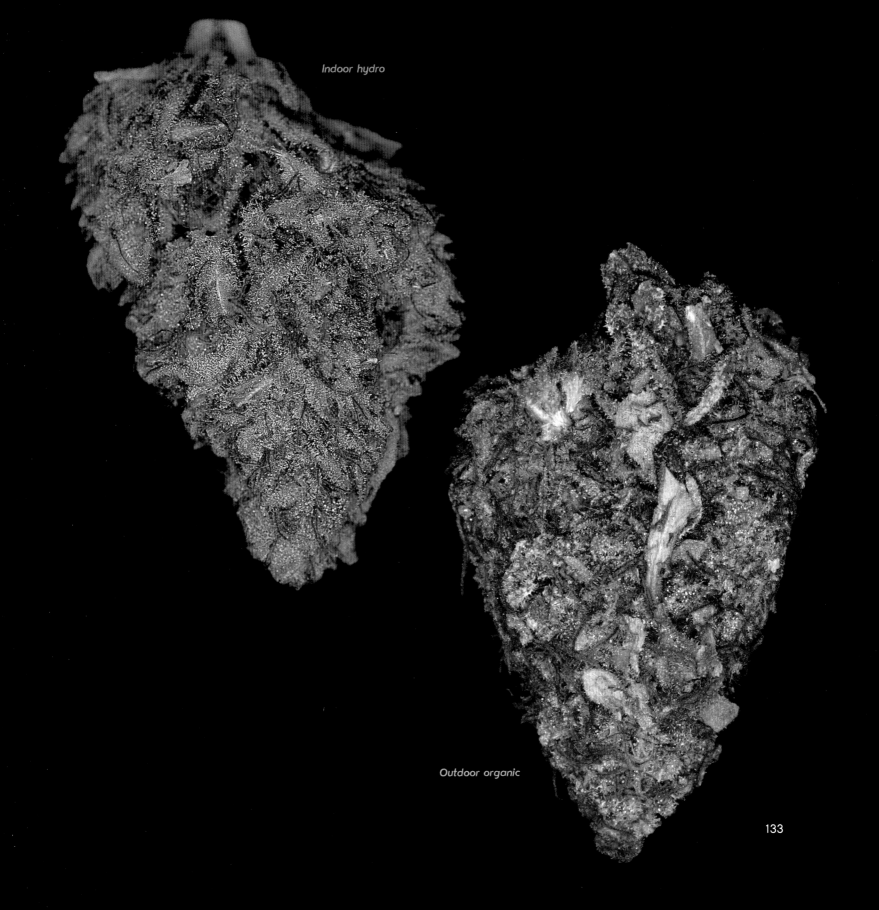

Indoor hydro

Outdoor organic

133

Live California outdoor Purps

The Purps

Here we have one of the most stunning strains I've ever experienced, **The Purps.** This strain, local to Northern California but extremely rare even there, had no weaknesses whatsoever. Aesthetically it is simply gorgeous. The smell, without even so much as a gentle squeeze, is damn near erotic: a combination of luscious grapes and nag champa incense, as well as a dozen other exotic notes. In fact, The Purps is considerably grapier than The Grape! (See page 68.) The flavor is earth-shatteringly delicious, tasting of grapes and nag champa even stronger than it smells! But most impressive is the high, a happy upbeat flight that really enabled me to see the positive in things. I noticed this every time I smoked it. Of course the grower's excellent vibe is equally responsible for this, but it's something that I noticed repeatedly with The Purps no matter who grew it. This is happy herb, and freakin' strong too! There is a noticeable antianxiety characteristic as well.

Lineage of The Purps isn't exactly clear. Judging by the growth pattern, it seems to be mostly indica. The flavor and high, however, seem more sativa oriented, possibly from Thai genetics. The strain came from two mystery seeds that were gifted to a lucky grower. Amazingly, they were twenty-three years old, last grown in 1977 in Northern California. One was a male that died. The other is what is now known as The Purps.

As someone who usually feels somewhat let down by the quality of today's purple ganja, I was more than pleasantly surprised to come across this royal strain. Easily the best purple bud

Hydro

Hydro

Outdoor organic

Outdoor California organic

136

I've tried, I would even go so far as to say that The Purps is among my top three favorite strains ever.

Two version of The Purps are shown, an indoor hydro versions, which was excellent and easily some of the finest hydro I've ever tried. The Thai flavor was very apparent, as well as deliciously spicy purple notes. But the outdoor organic California version was easily superior, with the grape and nag champa flavors powering through more than the Thai flavor in the hydro. I very much hope to see The Purps at a seed company soon.

One last thing about The Purps— there are four different phenotypes, even within the clone of this strain! I know it's bizarre and hard to accept, but there are four distinct possibilites of plant possible with a Purps clone. (Clones should in theory be exactly the same.) Even with 20 clones taken from the same mother and grown right next to each other, with identical conditions, four different types of plant, with different size, shape, color, and even flavor, will most likely be seen. The keeper of this strain, as well as many other people who have grown it, have attested to this strange fact. I have never seen another strain do this.

The Purps, cont'd

Salmon Creek Big Bud

A fairly common strain on the West Coast, **Salmon Creek Big Bud** is similar but not identical to the *real* Big Bud (which is different from Amsterdam Big Bud, which is different from B.C. Big Bud, and so on). She seems a little less weighty, and not quite as mediciney and dank tasting. Overall though, quite a nice smoke. These clones were grown organically indoors in soil in Humboldt, California.

137

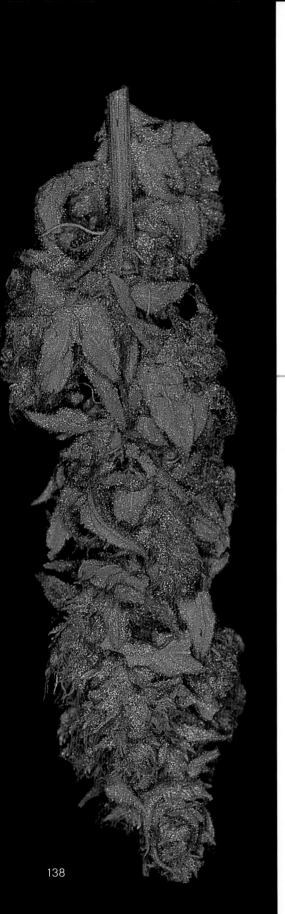

Sellwood Thunder

This twenty-year-old strain is from the Bobby B. collection (Bobby is an activist who won stoner of the month twice, whatever that means!). Coming from Portland, Oregon, this awesome, mostly indica strain has a complex flavor that is unique. With tangy persimmon high notes and a thick hashy undertone, the Thunder is very lush and exotic. The high is thick and euphoric; it made my entire chest cavity tingle. Some people say it helps with the disease fibromyalgia.

Shiva Shanti I

Although this strain was already shown in the first volume of *The Cannabible*, there were no acceptable live photos at that time. Here we have a lovely indoor, organic, soil-grown **Shiva Shanti I,** taken from old Sensi Seeds stock. These nugs were notable for their incredible denseness. Very garlicky and skunky, and a breeze to grow, these plants would do well in any indoor garden.

Indoor organic

Snow

Snow is an indica strain mostly seen in clone form on the West Coast of the U.S. I was surprised to learn just how many cannabis lovers put Snow at the top of their favorites list. Personally, although Snow is visually stunning, I found it to be quite bland and even boring. The flavor is a light sweetness with a faint glimmer of hashiness. Although it is above average in potency, I found the high to be a little dull, even generic. So many people get caught up in how "white" a strain is, but for me, it's all about the flavor and the high. (Indoor and outdoor versions shown.)

Oregon outdoor organic

Indoor

Sonic X Kush

This indoor, soil-grown, organic ganja comes from a skunky old Berkeley, California, sativa strain called **Sonic.** This strain was then crossed with a **Kush** indica plant, creating a hybrid that was quick, skunky, and potent. This sample was grown indoors in Hawaii, and due to the tropical, nutrient-rich air in the tropics, possessed a tropical tinge that was quite enjoyable.

The Munchies

It has been my observation that, for the average marijuana smoker, the most harmful effect of getting high is the massive pig-out that usually follows getting stoned. While appetite stimulation is highly desirable to certain people with illnesses, the average fat-assed American does not need to be eating refrigerators full of food every time they smoke a joint. This is no laughing matter. Overeating is a very unhealthy practice. When you consider the "foods" that most people gorge themselves on after getting stoned (candy, fried foods, dairy products, etc.) you will see my point. This has been a struggle for me, and despite the fact that I am very health conscious, I still struggle with overeating (when baked). I limit the damage to my body by only eating snacks from health-food stores, with no processed ingredients. The truth of the matter is, it doesn't matter how healthy the food you're eating is—if you're overeating, it's harmful to the body. This phenomenon led me to wonder whether it might be possible to breed a new strain of cannabis, selected for its low impact on appetite. It didn't take much research to learn that it's THC itself that so effectively stimulates the appetite. Breed that out of the plant, and you're smoking hemp! The real answer here is to learn self-discipline. One must convince oneself that it is just the munchies talking and that one is not *really* hungry. Or, one could rationalize and eat chocolate, claming that, since it has now been proven that eating chocolate can prolong a marijuana high, it will actually save a lot of money on herb (see page 35).

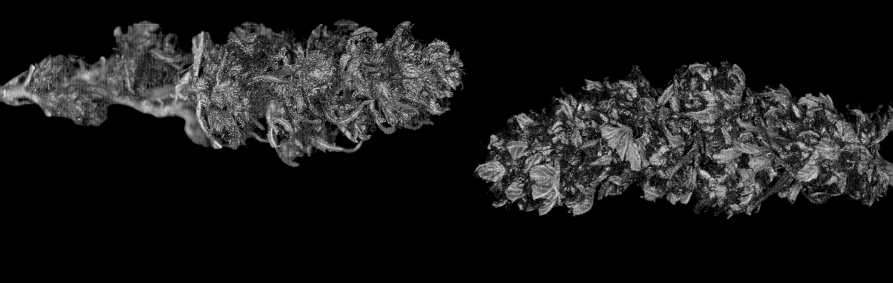

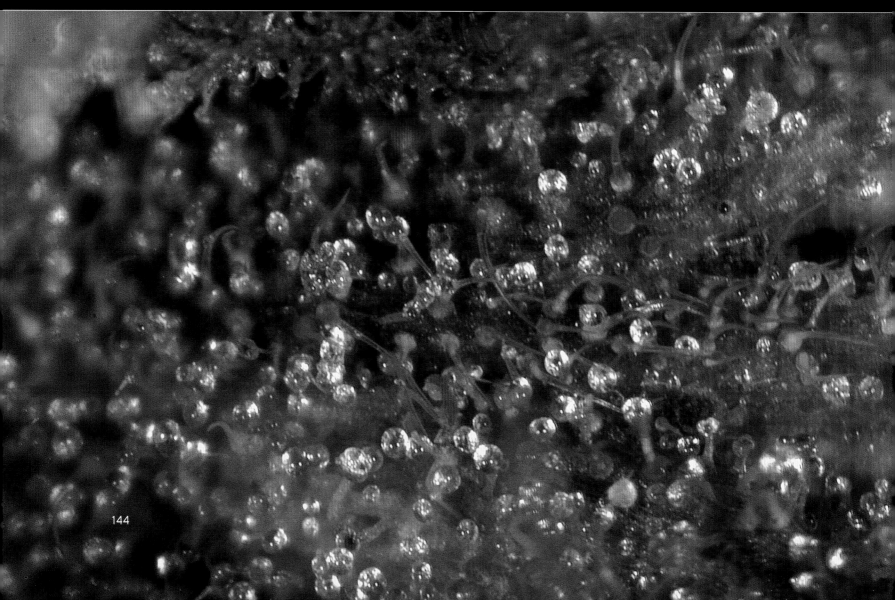

144

Spirit of 76

Coming from the hills of Mendocino County, California, **Spirit of 76** is an amazingly potent and beautiful plant. Capable of exhibiting every shade of purple imaginable, this mostly sativa packs a wallop of a stone that will impress even the most picky connoisseur. The high from this strain has made many a person change their plans for the day. Although the growth characteristic seems sativa dominated, the high seems very indica dominant. Thick and heavy, even numbing and spacey at times, Spirit of 76 can definitely take you on a ride. The flavor is very complex. Sandalwood, cherries, and fine hashish come to mind. Overall, a wonderful smoking experience.

Late season Spirit of 76

Spirit of 76

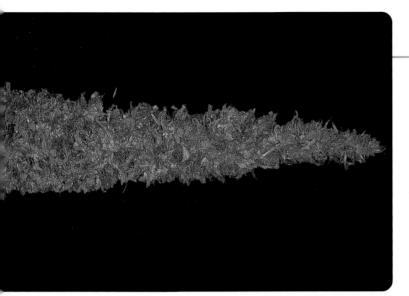

Starlight

Coming from the Super Skunky Seed Company, **Starlight,** as well as the rest of their strains, is a White Widow hybrid. They claim that all their strains are hybrid crosses with a White Widow male—questionable, since White Widow arrived in Amsterdam as a female clone. Either way, it is a nice strain, with a lovely fruity aroma suggesting strawberries. The high seems quite sativa oriented, clear, cerebral, and chatty.

147

Stone Blue

Northern California is the home to this fine, mostly indica strain, which has a beautiful hashy and piney flavor and aroma. The smoke is oh so smooth, and the high is no slouch either. Thick and penetrating, this outdoor-grown indica had me giggling and horizontal in a matter of minutes.

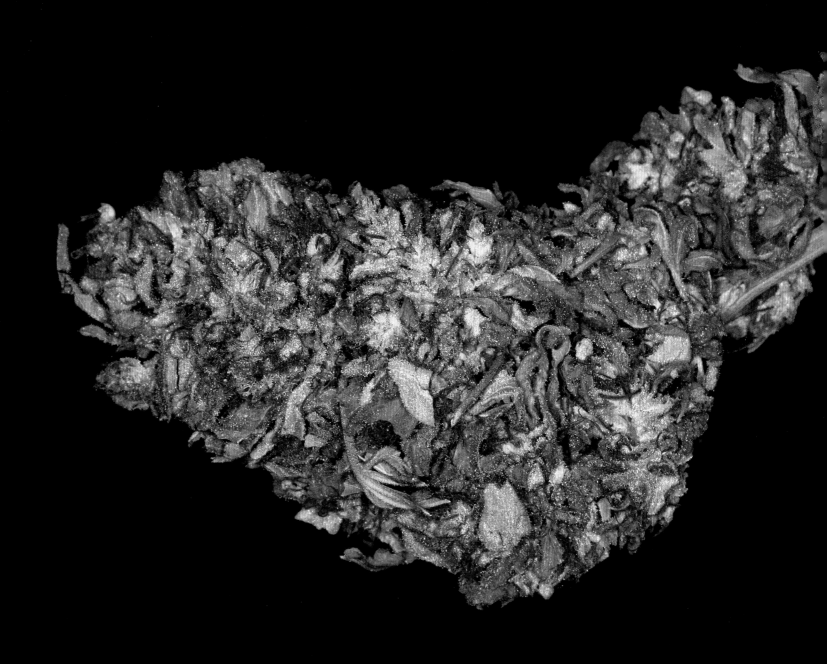

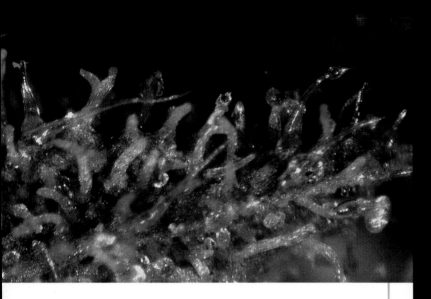

Sugar Baby

Another yummy Northern California strain, **Sugar Baby's** lineage is as follows: Orange Crush X G13/Blue Widow. Grown outdoors, "mostly" organically, the buds were creamy and sweet, with citrus tones on the exhalation. The high is moderate to strong, and felt mostly in the upper body and head.

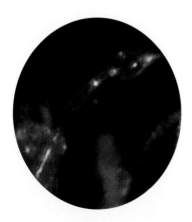

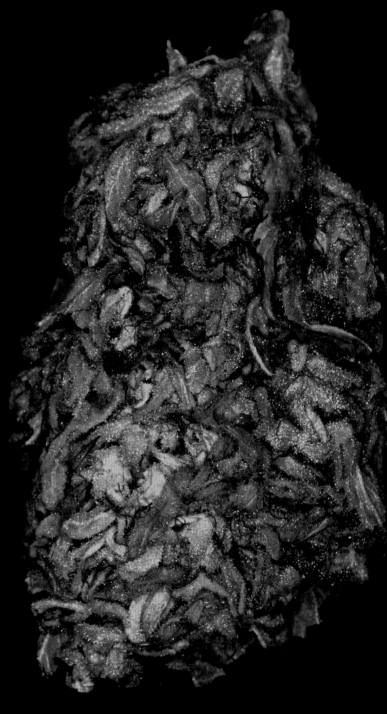

Super Dawg

Easily some of the finest hydroponically grown herb I've ever smoked, **Super Dawg** is a cross of an '86 Sensi Super Skunk and the Dawg. I reflected on how much better this was then any Super Skunk I've tried in Amsterdam, flavorful beyond description. There is a wide array of flavors in this one, ranging from acrid skunky to tropical petrol. The high, in one word—intense!

151

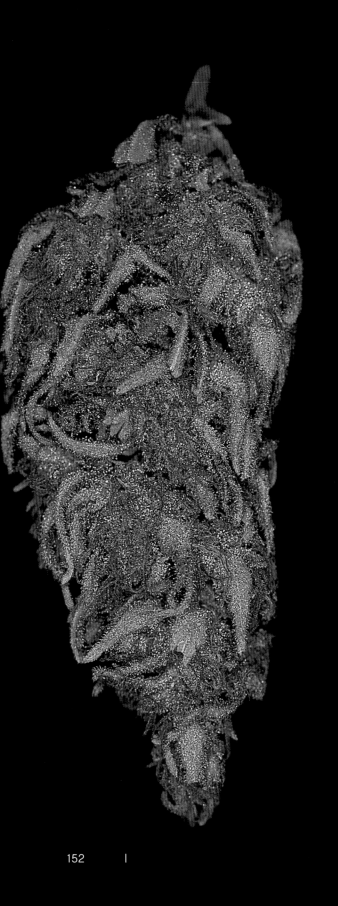

Super Silver Haze

Well, I asked for it in the first volume of *The Cannabible*. And here we have it. Outdoor organic **Super Silver Haze,** grown in the intense California sun. No problems with a joint staying lit here, as was and is so often the case with Amsterdam indoor-grown herb. This deliciously spicy ganja was extremely earthy and produced a clear high that, although very strong, was not of the couch-locking variety. My compliments to the grower of this fine herb. The first volume of *The Cannabible* has the Amsterdam indoor version of this Cannabis Cup–winning strain.

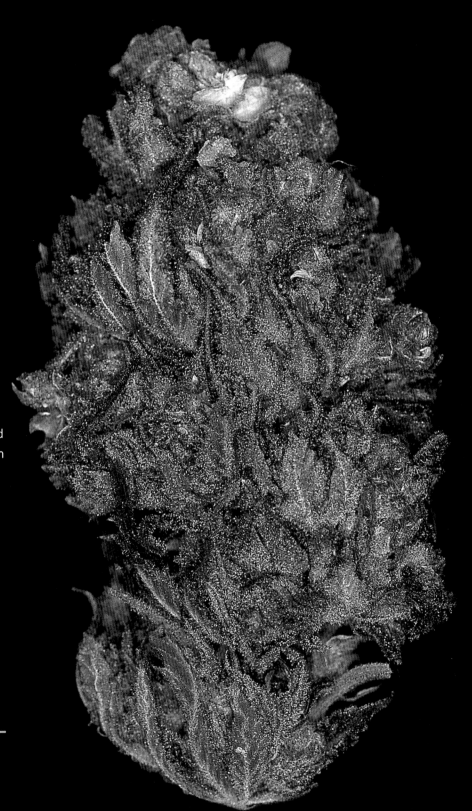

Sweet Skunk

This is reportedly a rare sativa that Breeder
Steve discovered in the early '90s. She smells and
tastes about as sweet as possible, and gets even
sweeter with age. The high is a perfect balance
of cerebral and body action. This particular
batch was grown organically indoors in soil. She
has a scrumptious, tropical, pungent quality,
almost but not quite hazy. The flavor is actually
quite complex—pungent on the inhale, super-
sweet on the exhale. It's almost like an overripe
mango, with thick skunky tones as well. This one
definitely tastes as good as it smells. The high is
intense yet manageable, hitting right behind the
third eye. Absolutely tasty till the roach burns
your fingers. Fifty-seven-day flowering time.

These gigantic plants harvested several pounds a piece.

Sweet Swiss

This breathtaking Swiss sativa was grown organically outdoors in Northern California. These days, she's called **"Sweet Swiss"** but was known before that as the "Heaven's Gate" or "Grand Flora," both loose translations of the original Swiss name. Floral and spicy, she reminded me of an old Colombian-Mexican hybrid. The high is energetic, cerebral, and quite nice.

Sweet Tooth

Sweet Tooth is a Spice of Life Seeds strain that I am quite impressed with. It comes from the Sweet Pink Grapefruit and Blueberry genetic pools, and Breeder Steve's selecting skills are right on. This mostly indica is almost too sweet, but if you like sweet-tasting herb, you can't go wrong. This fat-bracted plant is prone to developing stunning purple accents on the calyxes and produces acceptably heavy plants. Two different batches of Sweet Tooth are shown: one indoor organic batch and one California outdoor batch. Both were excellent.

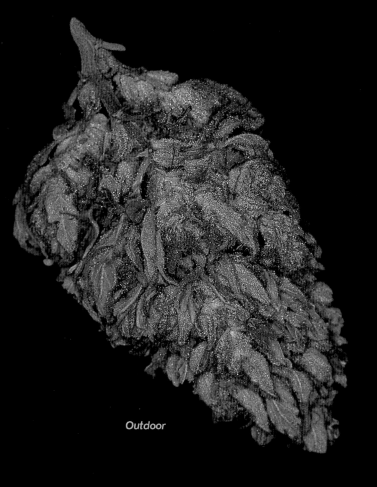

Outdoor

Indoor

155

Switzerland

this diverse array of gorgeous ganja was all grown in Switzerland by an American named Chris Iverson, who is apparently one of the only Americans to go to Switzerland and pull this type of feat off. All the plants are grown completely organically, and in full sunlight (well, as much as one can get in Switzerland), and the quality is surprisingly good. To be honest, much of the herb grown in Switzerland is of mediocre quality, so I was very pleased to see some fine herb coming out of this awesomely beautiful country. I would match the quality to a good Californian selection.

Chris is currently putting the finishing touches on his movie *The Green Goddess*, which is based on this experience. Check it out (www.greengoddess.info).

OPPOSITE:

bottom left:
Kryptomania

bottom right:
Citral 3

156

157

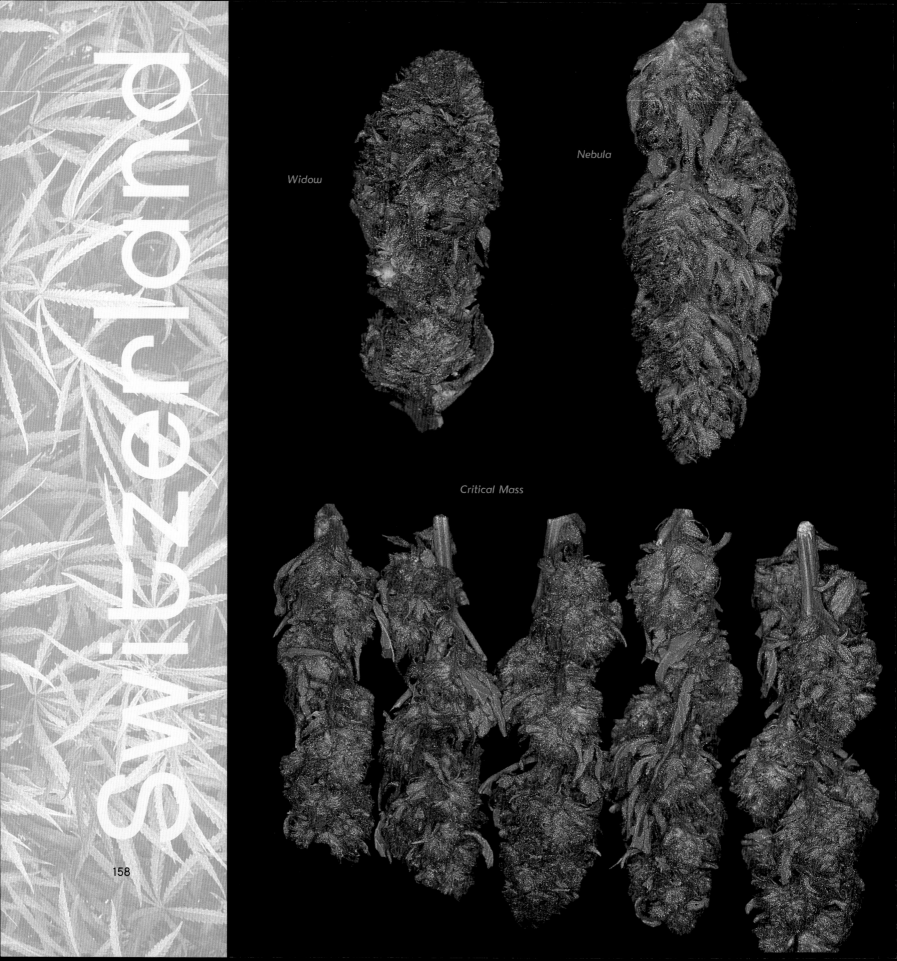

Widow

Nebula

Critical Mass

Durga Mata

Amsterdam Flame

Black Domina

Bubble Gum

Kryptomania

159

The Swiss Experience

For the last ten years, Switzerland has been at the forefront of policy making and progressive thinking when it comes to cannabis. To the Swiss, it's all hemp—on one level, there is no differentiation made between cannabis used for medicine and cannabis for pants. This is very important, as it deglamorizes the whole "marijuana phenomenon." (In America, it's funny yet sad to watch dread-locked stoners trying to promote hemp and claiming, "No, this isn't about getting high! We just want to wear durable clothes, dude!") Switzerland is a very misunderstood place, and its state of constant change makes it even less understood. I will now attempt to describe and clarify the situation.

In 1994, a woman named Shirin Patterson started Swihtco, the Swiss Hemp Trading Company. At this same time, a Swiss lawyer named Jean-Pierre Egger discovered that growing hemp with THC was never made illegal, because the Swiss never signed the same international drug treaties that almost every other country on earth caved into and signed. Unfortunately, Patterson had no experience with hemp, so she made the logical choice of going to Amsterdam to seek help. She returned with thousands of seeds of some of Amsterdam's top strains, only to then cross them with schwaggy local Swiss hemp strains. This way, when asked, she could tell people that it was local Swiss hemp. Thereby the now infamous Swiss Mix (or Swiss miss!) was created. Unfortunately, no matter how good the Amsterdam strains were, once "low" hybridized with Swiss hemp, at best they would produce weak and bland herb. Patterson promoted and sold these seeds fervently, telling farmers that they were legal high-quality Swiss strains, and unfortunately, most of the Swiss farmers bought the half-hemp. The ripple of this experience can still be felt today, and it set Switzerland's herb scene back several years. Even *High Times* magazine dissed Swiss herb, claiming none of it got them high.

At this point, despite the crappy genetics and bad publicity, the Swiss hemp scene exploded. Shops popped up everywhere, selling everything from grow lights to "tea" and "aromatherapy pillows" (which was essentially a hemp-cloth pillowcase stuffed full of buds, available in various qualities and sizes). This was the first tolerated form of sales and distribution of "hemp" within Switzerland. Although these pillows were occasionally used by legitimate asthma sufferers, most of them were torn open and rolled into what I call Eurospleefs, huge joints containing some herb and a bunch of nasty chemically grown tobacco (Switzerland has the highest tobacco use in Europe).

Many Swiss farmers were attracted to hemp, and live plants became a common sight at local farmer's markets. By the year 2000, thousands of hectares of Swiss "hemp" were being grown, most of which was unfortunately still coming from the Swiss Mix seed stock. At the same time, marijuana experts from around the world were hearing of the opportunities in Switzerland and showing up with new genetics and ideas. It was only a matter of time before the new genetics had their effect, and soon Switzerland started producing some quality herb.

The police in Switzerland are very intelligent and professional. People very rarely go to jail for cannabis. A notable exception to this was Bernard Rappaz, a Swiss man who was caught with an astonishing forty tons of cannabis, as well as five hundred kilos of top-quality hashish (tested at 45 percent THC). Even more astonishing than that was his over eighty day hunger strike while in jail. He is now free.

With tolerance and forward thinking, the Swiss government has allowed this cannabis experiment to happen, in the hopes of avoiding the casualties that come along with American-style drug war tactics. As of this writing, there are over 500 hemp stores in Switzerland, most of which are selling ganja openly. Usually it is sold in plastic bags sealed with a note saying, "Do not open or smoke this hemp. It is to be used for aromatherapy only."

Only time will tell where this will all end up, but it seems as though complete legalization is right around the corner.

Hash Plant

161

TC Blu

TC Blu, or "Trinity County Blueberry," is a favorite among cannisseurs in the Pacific Northwest, especially in Eugene, Oregon. This extremely phat plant was created by crossing a DJ Short Blueberry male to the legendary Trinity female (see page 170). The results are a thick, juicy plant with overpowering fruity and skunky tones of flavor. The high is quite worthy as well, a full-bodied, spine-tingling, ass-kicking buzz that would please any cannabis lover. This particular batch was grown organically indoors in soil, in Eugene, Oregon, where TC Blu is most often seen.

162

Texada Timewarp

Here we have a lovely live plant of the famous **Texada Timewarp,** a Canadian sativa originating on Texada Island, which is in the Georgia Strait. This clone comes from a twenty-year-old mother, therefore only crosses are available in seed form. She was grown outdoors organically in Humboldt, California, and has a superbly perfumed flowery aroma and flavor. The high is very nice, cerebral, and active in the frontal lobes especially.

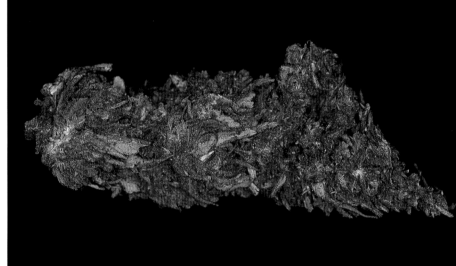

Thai

Here we have arguably the best **Thai** bud I've ever tried. Grown outdoors in California, these one-year-old-plus sativa buds have a wicked Thai flavor that is exquisite. Similar to anise mixed with a light tarry tobacco, the flavor just seems to get better and better as the joint progresses. But the high is where a good Thai will really stand out. Soaring and trippy, even psychedelic at times, this bud was much better than what can now be found for the most part in Thailand, unfortunately.

Thai X Haze

This exquisite sativa cross was grown organically outdoors in full sunlight in Grass Valley, California. The flavor is the typical Thai thing, which is hard to describe, because it is unique. It resembles a tarry light tobacco, with a citrus and spice over-tone. It's extremely earthy and rich, an absolute joy to puff. It's amazing that this bud is so dense, considering its **Thai** and **Haze** parents are not at all known for being dense. The high of this strain is also very impressive, a psychedelic and clear upward spiraling buzz that is not at all debilitating, as many of today's indicas are.

Trainwreck

Another favorite among West Coast connoisseurs, **Trainwreck** is a vitaminy lemon-lime spicy sativa that produces a racy and very "up" high that is quite productive and enjoyable. Trainwreck buds are usually very dense, with clawlike pods, and almost no leaf at all. The smell of this exquisite herb is intoxicating in itself. Several deep inhalations in a jar of organic Trainwreck will have a sedative effect on almost anyone. Unfortunately the strain has a hermaphroditic quality, and male flowers can easily be spotted on any batch of the 'wreck. Still, the strain is excellent and commonly found in connoisseur circles of Northern California. Several batches, both indoor and outdoor, are shown on the following two pages. It's fascinating to see all of the different batches, knowing that they are all exactly the same clones, but grown by different people.

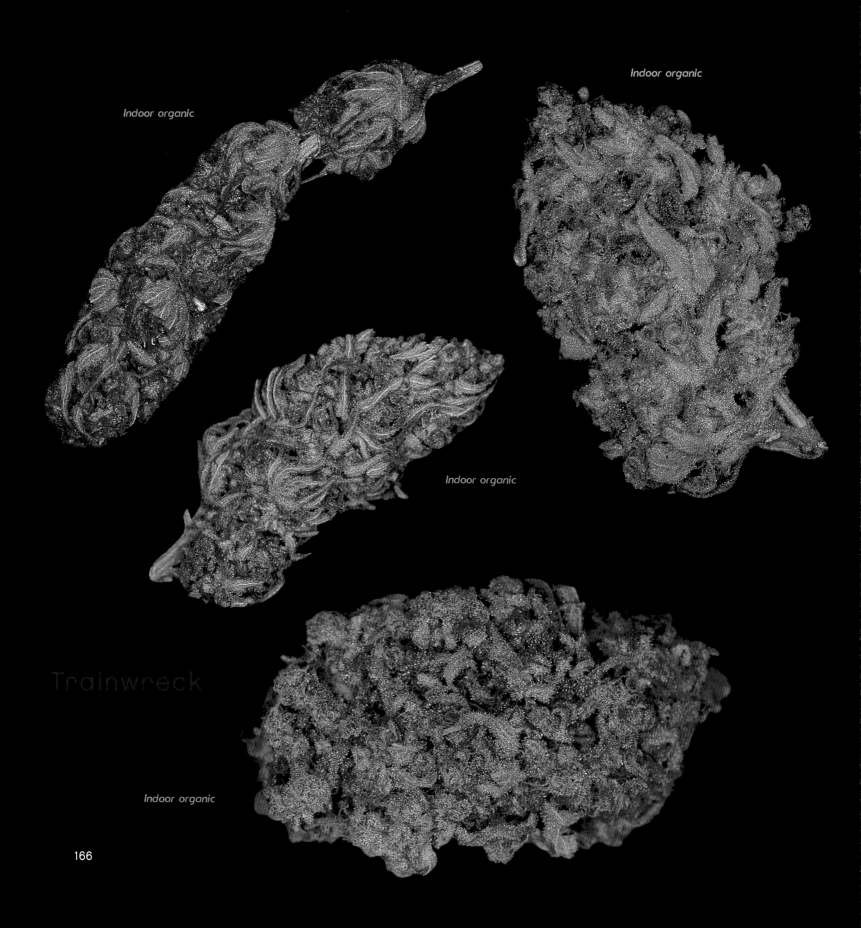

Indoor organic

Indoor organic

Indoor organic

Trainwreck

Indoor organic

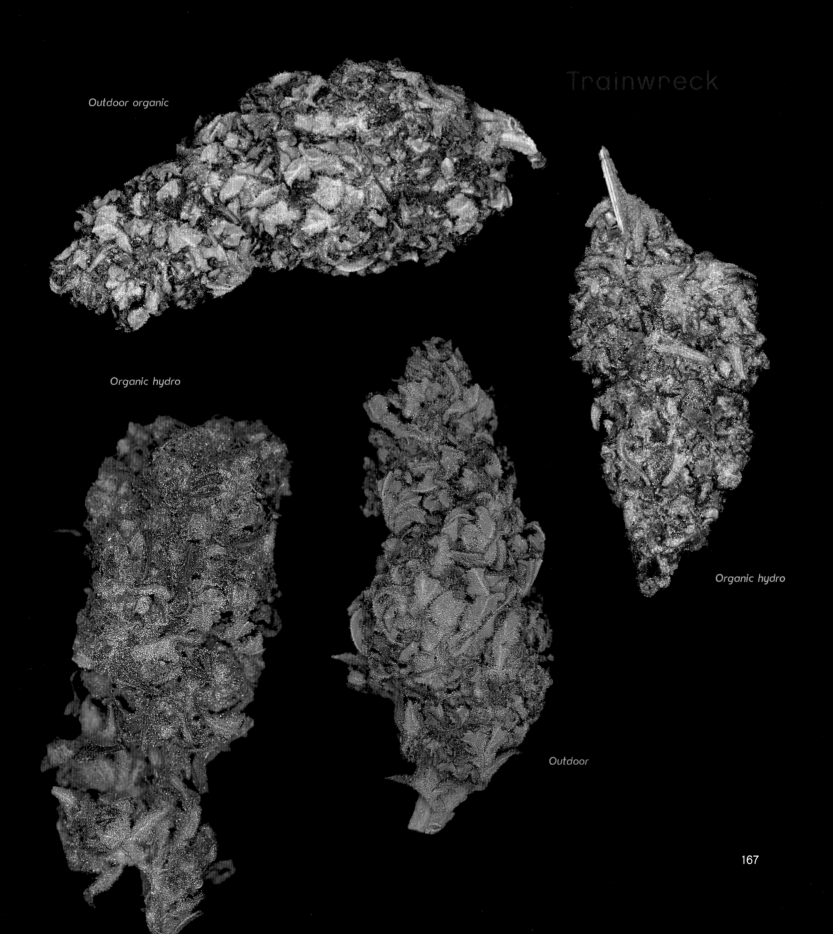

Trainwreck

Outdoor organic

Organic hydro

Organic hydro

Outdoor

Trainwreck stems

Trainwreck

Invoking the Spirit of the Plant

With so many strains and so many growers, it is no wonder there is such a variety of smoke available to us all. In the fine-tuning of the Kind, we begin to notice a difference between the same strain grown by two different people living in the same town, using the same method. How does this happen? How could one person grow Mothership and another grow what turns out to be a lesser version of the same clone known as the Othership? Could it be that this female plant responds best to a female cultivator? Maybe one of the growers had a rough, stressful, and paranoid personal life between harvests. All this is possible, yet if you pay close attention, you will notice something else going on.

It is interesting to note that a cultivator, say Bob, can grow several different strains, yet each will be recognizable as Bob's herb. It is not just the fertilizers or lights that Bob uses—it's Bob's energy being expressed through the plant. For example, I know a grower, let's again say Bob, whose many strains all carry a particularly unique purple, spicy, and creamy flavor. Each various strain in his vast collection is individually recognizable, yet it is all very obviously "Bob herb."

If you took ten clones from the same plant and gave them to ten different growers, you would very likely see ten very different samples when all was said and done. This will happen even when multiple growers are using the exact same setup, even in the same town (see Trainwreck, pages 165–68, for multiple examples from the same clone).

So, what I'm getting at is that the personal essence of the grower, their "vibe," has much to do with the resulting harvest. For example, I've never met anyone who has tried real Big Sur Holy Nugs that didn't think it was the finest herb they ever smoked. This legendary herb was said to have been grown by monks who meditated and prayed with the plants daily. Is it possible that their high vibration had an effect on the ganja they grew? I believe so.

In addition, another level can be applied. Upon closer examination, you may find that the Othership grower has yet to develop a spiritual connection with the plant. Often, in the beginning stages of cultivation of a strain, the grower needs to take time to get to know all of the particular needs and the creative expression of the plant. This connection can be deeply enhanced with lovingly enthusiastic communication. This may be done verbally, with the caregiver singing praises to the lovely green ladies. It may come about through an attentive touch and awareness to details. Most effectively, a grower can learn to invoke the spirit of the plant through receiving its messages. While meditating with, smelling, smoking, vaporizing, eating, or ingesting the herb in any other way, the masterful cultivators will learn to synergize themselves with the unique essence of the herb and will in turn be more able to help bring forth its ultimate beauty. This method of blending with the plant and then lovingly invoking its essence to return in the new form is humankind communing with nature at its highest and best.

Trinity

I have recently learned that **Trinity,** an
extremely popular and sought-after strain in
the Pacific Northwest, originally comes from
Kansas of all places. This 65 percent sativa is
an original Skunk #1 crossed with a mystery
indica, according to reputable sources. The
stuff is so ridiculously skunky that it can't be
contained—not recommended for growers
with close neighbors. And I'm not referring to
Amsterdam skunky, which is actually sweet.
I'm talking about roadkill skunky. The high is
quite strong and up, great for deep,
thought-provoking conversations. This batch
was grown organically indoors in soil and
was extremely tasty.

BOTTOM RIGHT: *Outdoor Trinity X U Dub*

Trip (Big Sur Holy Nug) X Killer Queen

Trip, according to what I learned, is another name for the legendary Big Sur Holy weed. This herb was supposedly grown by Buddhist monks in Northern California around twenty-five years ago, and legends about its astounding quality still exist. **Killer Queen** is a cross of G13 and Cinderella 99. This bud had sublime tanginess, very expanding, with hints of diesel and fine Afghani hashish. Soon there was a powerful mind-numbing thump felt in the upper body and especially in the back of the head. The intense and unique flavor made me wonder if Diesel came from these genetics.

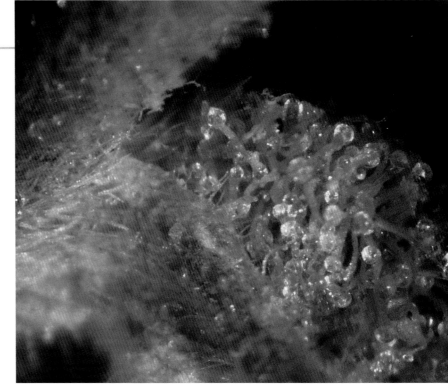

Tropical Mist

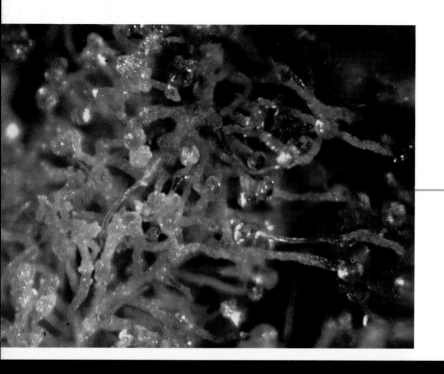

Coming out of Portland, Oregon, **Tropical Mist** is a hybridized cross of Sensi Star and Kali Mist. She has a penetrating, fruity, tropical tinge that is just superb. This strain is very appropriately named. The high was equally impressive, a pleasant and very thorough tingling sensation that could be felt everywhere, but especially right behind the third eye. This one was grown organically indoors in soil.

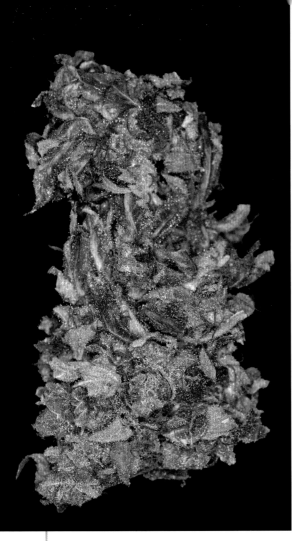

U Dub

This indica strain reportedly comes from medical cannabis research done in the '70s at the University of Washington. The strain is quite dank and actually has a very mediciney flavor. The high is thick and powerful—I noticed my heart beating harder in my chest.

Williams Wonder

Although **Williams Wonder** was
already shown in the first volume of
The Cannabible, this bud was completely different (and better) than the
first version, and therefore needed to be
seen. It is highly unfortunate that a
photo cannot convey an aroma or flavor, because this nugget has a bouquet
that is simply intoxicating—possibly
erotic. Tangy and fruity, but a completely
different tang and fruitiness than other
strains have. I couldn't stop smelling it!
Willies Wonder is mostly a sativa, and
comes from the legendary SSSC, Super
Sativa Seed Club. This batch was grown
organically indoors in soil.

Wonder

I picked up this gorgeous nug at the Seattle Hemp Fest. I was very pleased, as both the flavor and high were fantastic. Grown organically indoors in soil, this relatively new strain had a lovely light and dusty sandalwood flavor, with pleasing "affy" undertones. She balances out at 60 percent indica, 40 percent sativa and packs a strong buzz that would satisfy any connoisseur.

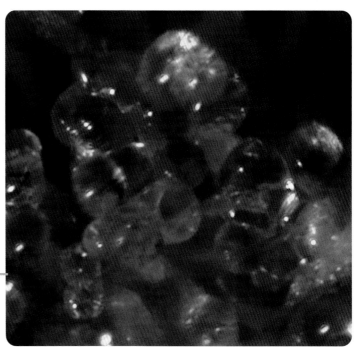

The Hawaii Cannabis Ministry

BY ROGER CHRISTIE

 Would you like to be free of the legal problems associated with cannabis for the rest of your life?

 Could you benefit from personal identification that will help to protect you from arrest, prosecution, and conviction on cannabis charges?

 Do you use cannabis religiously?

 Would you like to use cannabis religiously?

 Are you over eighteen years of age?

If you answered yes to any of these questions, then membership in the Hawaiian Cannabis Ministry (THC Ministry) might just be for you. THC Ministry is an exercise in personal and spiritual empowerment. I help take negative energy and turn it positive.

Personally and spiritually, THC Ministry is about empowerment of the individual. My intention is that each and every one of us who prays for legal cannabis gets his or her prayer answered in the positive. Once you know the good news, you become stronger in your faith and feel better about yourself. Guilt, fear, shame, and other doubts begin to melt away.

What do I mean by saying that we use cannabis "religiously"? The term *religiously* has more than one meaning. I use it to mean that we use cannabis respectfully, consciously, prayerfully. And I mean that we use it regularly, as a sacrament.

There is historical evidence for the view of cannabis as a sacrament that becomes stronger every day, suggesting that cannabis was the original sacrament of the Hindu, Shinto, Hebrew, Christian, and Rasta religions. Cannabis is the burning bush, the tree of life, the plant of renown, the premier sustainable natural resource on earth to take care of most of our physical and spiritual hungers. God, that's great! So many blessings in one plant.

Many people have said over the years that the most dangerous thing about cannabis is its illegality and that a person could go to jail for its cultivation or its use. That has been true for *way* too long. In my opinion, despite all the greed, negativity, and tragedy, the prohibition of cannabis hemp can be an opportunity for personal and spiritual redemption. It's a challenge, and it's an opportunity to grow. The extreme prohibition of our holy sacrament actually enables us to claim and access part of our "divine inheritance" from the creator of all.

A few years ago I got tired and frustrated working and waiting for the legalization of marijuana to happen. Enough already! I personally couldn't wait another second. I *had* to do something creative to secure the place of cannabis in my life—and I did. I applied and studied and was ordained into a cannabis sacrament ministry here on the Big Island called the Religion of Jesus Church in June of 2000. That same month I received my license to perform marriages in the state of Hawaii, specifically as a "cannabis sacrament" minister. I hold minister's license number 00-313, issued by the state of Hawaii Department of Health. Among other things, my license is "reasonable doubt" in the mind of any jury in the land for cannabis.

Someday cannabis might become legal in the United States and in all other nations. I sure hope that it does. Until then, I offer the Hawaii Cannabis Ministry to help you legally defend your religious use of cannabis as sacrament under the protections of the U.S. First Amendment and under international law. It's a proactive approach, and it works. In all the cases that I know of, THC Ministry has successfully helped people defend themselves in court. As far as I know, our paperwork has succeeded 100 percent of the time it has been used, an amazing track record backed up by testimonials. See the website (www.thc-ministry.org) for details. We have over 18,000 people now with our paperwork, so that's saying a lot for this method of communication and our proactive approach.

THC Ministry paperwork and formula are legally called a "defense to prosecution," and they're working very well in every state where they have been tested, even at the U.S.-Canadian border with the U.S. Customs Service. There is a legal precedent called the "Andrews Test," in State v. Blake, that says that a person can use an otherwise prohibited substance for religious purposes if they can meet the test. Here are the requirements. If you are sincere, if you are legitimate, if your use of the sacrament is mandatory for your religious practice, if you use the sacrament in private, and if you are not in commerce with the sacrament, then you can qualify for a "defense to prosecution" when others would be prosecuted—sincere, legitimate, mandatory, private, religion, not commerce.

The Hawaii Cannabis Ministry is the answer to my prayer for legal cannabis in my life. If this point of view appeals to you, it can help to answer your prayer for legal cannabis in your life—today.

With all my love,
Roger Christie
February 7, 2003
Hilo, Kingdom of Hawaii
The Hawaii Cannabis Ministry
"We use cannabis religiously and you can, too."
www.thc-ministry.org
(808) 961-0488

Afterword

a s I sit here, just days before *The Cannabible 2* goes to the publisher, I reflect on all that's happened in the last year since the first *Cannabible* came out. I've met so many incredible beings who have inspired me and become lifelong friends. All the wonderful people I meet in my travels are the best part about my job (the herb is pretty fantastic too!). Proposition 215 and all the other medical marijuana initiatives have greatly helped my quest, yet the list of strains that I have not photographed still rapidly grows. People have contacted me from all over the world, inviting me to photograph their local delicacies. For *The Cannabible 3*, my preliminary plan is to visit Australia, New Zealand, Alaska, Greenland, Africa (including Lesotho, Swaziland, South Africa, and Malawi), and of course more of the U.S. mainland and Hawaii. I also plan on writing a seed breeder's edition, featuring only strains that can be purchased from seed companies, as well as an edition dedicated to landraces. A very respectable chunk of what California has to offer was covered in this volume, but there is still so much more. To be honest, the job's almost intimidating. Much as I love to puff, my body is strongly requesting an extensive ganja fast, so I will oblige. But then it's back to work. Lots of people think they have the best job in the world, but I know that I do. Thank you so much for helping me to truly make this dream a reality.

Recommended Reading

Cannabis Books

The Benefits of Marijuana: Physical, Psychological, and Spiritual, by Joan Bello

A Brief History of Drugs: From the Stone Age to the Stoned Age, by Antonio Escohotado

The Emperor Wears No Clothes, by Jack Herer

Hashish!, by Robert Connell Clarke

Marijuana Botany, by Robert Connell Clarke

Marijuana Chemistry, by Michael Starks

Mr. Nice, by Howard Marks

This Is Cannabis, by Nick Brownlee

Health Books

Conscious Eating, by Gabriel Cousins

Diet for a New America, by John Robbins

Eating Alive, by John Matsen

Fast Food Nation: The Dark Side of the All-American Meal, by Eric Schlosser

The Healing Energies of Water, by Charlie Ryrie

Living Energies, by Callum Coats

Sunfood Diet Success System, by David Wolfe

Miscellaneous Books

Acid Dreams: The Complete Social History of LSD: The CIA, the Sixties, and Beyond, by Martin A. Lee and Bruce Shlain

And the Truth Shall Set You Free, by David Icke

The Celestine Prophecy, by James Redfield

Conversations with God, by Neal Donald Walsh

The New Taste of Chocolate, by Maricel E. Presilla

The Power of Now, by Eckhart Tolle

Secret Life of Nature, by Peter Tompkins

Secret Life of Plants, by Peter Tompkins and Christopher Bird

Secrets of the Soil, by Peter Tompkins and Christopher Bird

Index